name?

Fiona

— the Irish meaning is white and the Scottish, beautiful child variations Fee, Finella, Finola, Fionna

Kylie

— Australian aboriginal for boomerang it's a one-off

Gina

— means garden variations Geena, Ginat, Georgina

Lucy

— from Lucia which means glittering other variations are Lucille, Lucinda, Lulu, Cindy

Mariah

— a form of Mary, child of our wishes variations include Maria, Marietta, Mimi, Molly, Polly.

Katie

— from Catherine, meaning pure other variations include Kathleen, Katy, Karen

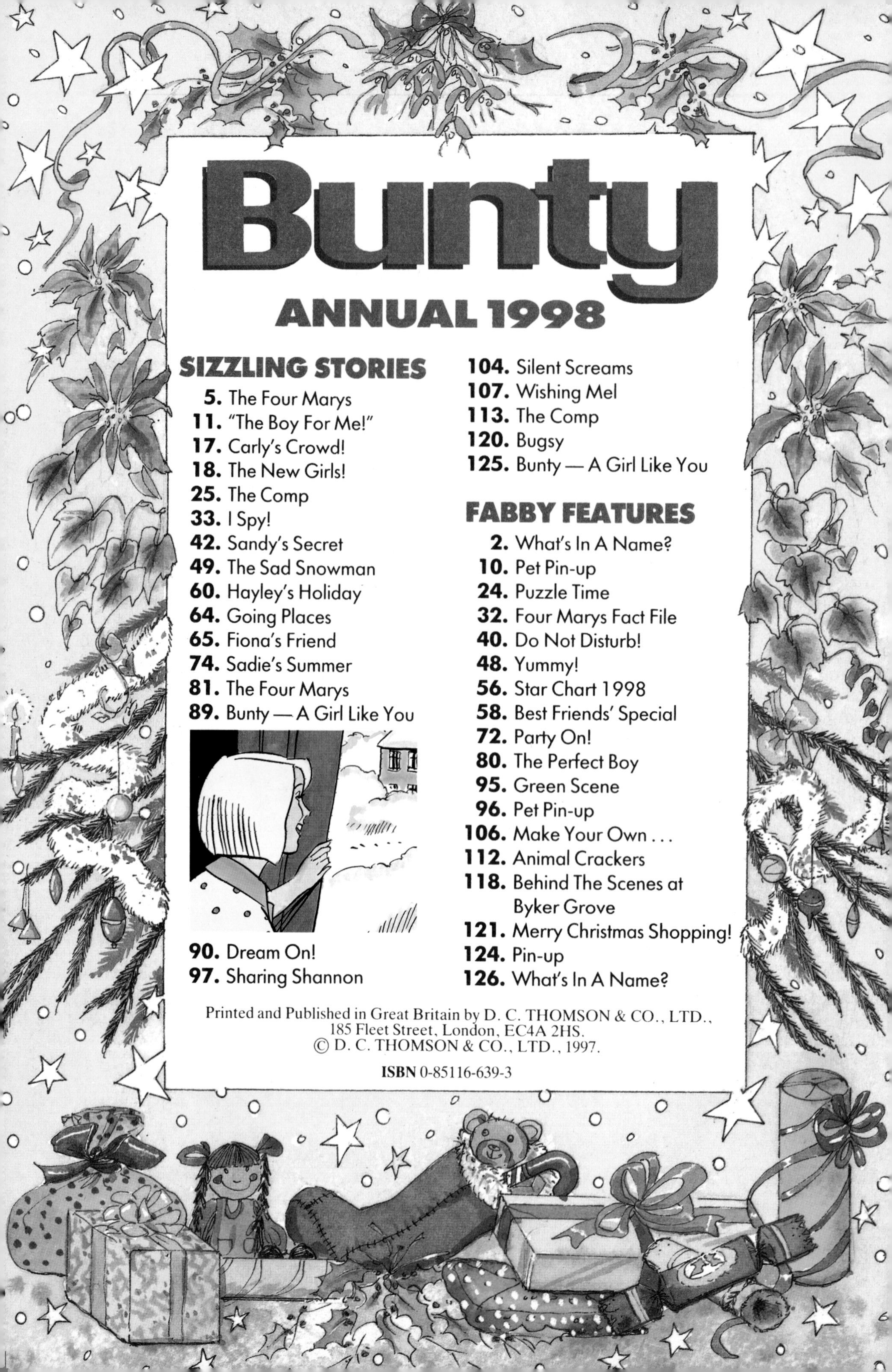

Bunty

ANNUAL 1998

SIZZLING STORIES

FABBY FEATURES

Printed and Published in Great Britain by D. C. THOMSON & CO., LTD.,
185 Fleet Street, London, EC4A 2HS.

ISBN 0-85116-639-3

The Four Marys

Miss Creef agreed and, soon —
WOW, THE SKY'S DARK, ISN'T IT? I THINK WE'RE IN FOR A REALLY HEAVY SNOWSTORM.
I HOPE SO. A WHITE CHRISTMAS WOULD BE GREAT — AS LONG AS IT DOESN'T STOP US GETTING HOME FOR THE HOLIDAYS, THAT IS.
Then —
LOOK AT THIS HOLLY, COTTY, IT'S PERFECT. THERE ARE *LOADS* OF BERRIES ON IT.
GREAT! LET'S GET CUTTING THEN. I WANT TO GET BACK TO SCHOOL BEFORE THE SNOW GETS ANY HEAVIER.
Meanwhile —
BAD NEWS, I'M AFRAID, MISS CREEF. MR JENNINGS CRASHED HIS VAN ON THE ICY ROADS THIS MORNING. HE ISN'T BADLY HURT, BUT HE WON'T BE ABLE TO DELIVER THE PRESENTS AS WE PLANNED.
OH, NO! THE PARTY WON'T BE THE SAME WITHOUT SANTA.
YOU'RE RIGHT. LET'S GO AND MEET COTTY AND FIELDY AND TELL THEM THE BAD NEWS.
So —
WE'LL HAVE TO FIND ANOTHER WAY TO HAND OUT THE PRESSIES. MAYBE WE COULD GET THE JUNIOR GIRLS TO DRESS UP AS ELVES AND . . .
LOOK, RADDY! WHO-WHO'S THAT?
CALM DOWN, SIMPY, IT'S ONLY MR JARVIS, THE GAMEKEEPER. I EXPECT HE'S JUST CHECKING UP ON THINGS BEFORE THE BAD WEATHER SETS IN.
HELLO, GIRLS. HAVE A NICE CHRISTMAS.
Deeper in the woods —
STOP, FIELDY! THERE'S A BABY DEER OVER THERE. KEEP STILL OR WE'LL FRIGHTEN IT.
IT MUST HAVE STRAYED FROM THE DEER PARK.

IT'S SEEN US, BUT IT'S NOT MOVING.
MABYE IT'S INJURED. LET'S TAKE A CLOSER LOOK.
But —
IT'S NOT INJURED — IT'S *TRAPPED!* LOOK, THERE'S A TYPE OF ROPE SNARE ROUND ITS LEG.
OH, THE POOR LITTLE THING. LET'S GET IT FREE.

Suddenly —
WELL, WELL, LOOKS LIKE WE'VE CAUGHT OURSELVES A DEER, TERRY.
WHAT?

IT'S NOTHIN' TO DO WITH YOU, SO KEEP YOUR NOSE OUT OF IT.
YEAH! WE'LL SEE TO THE DEER NOW.

I'M SCARED, FIELDY. WHO DO YOU THINK THEY ARE?
I DON'T KNOW, BUT WE *CAN'T* LET THEM TAKE THE DEER.

Then —
HERE YOU ARE, WE . . . OH!
NOT *MORE* OF 'EM! CLEAR OFF, THE LOT OF YOU!
THEY'RE *POACHERS!* SHOUT, GIRLS! MR JARVIS MIGHT HEAR US.

So —
HELP! MR JARVIS!
PRETENDING SOMEBODY'S THERE, ARE YOU? HUH! WE'RE NOT STUPID ENOUGH TO FALL FOR *THAT* OLD TRICK.
POACHERS! HELP! MR JARVIS.

NO REPLY. HE-HE MUST BE TOO FAR AWAY.
THAT MEANS THE MEN WILL GET AWAY WITH THE DEER. THERE'S NO WAY *WE* CAN STOP THEM.

But —
OH! HERE HE COMES NOW! THANK GOODNESS.
COME ON, TERRY. LET'S GET OUT OF HERE.
OI! YOU TWO! WHAT'S GOING ON?

I KNOW THOSE TWO AND I'LL CATCH UP WITH THEM LATER. FIRST, I WANT TO SEE TO THIS LITTLE CHAP AND GET HIM BACK TO THE DEER PARK. YOU CAN COME ALONG AND TELL THE OWNERS HOW YOU FOUND HIM.

So —
WE'RE VERY GRATEFUL TO YOU. THANK YOU *VERY* MUCH, GIRLS.

ARE ALL YOUR DEER THE SAME, MRS SHERWOOD?
NO, WE HAVE SEVERAL DIFFERENT BREEDS HERE. NOW, COME TO THE HOUSE AND HAVE SOMETHING TO EAT AND A HOT DRINK. YOU MUST BE FROZEN.

Soon —
EAT UP, GIRLS. AND, REMEMBER, IF THERE'S EVER ANYTHING WE CAN DO TO HELP YOUR SCHOOL, *PLEASE* LET US KNOW. WE REALLY *ARE* IN YOUR DEBT, YOU KNOW.

WELL, ACTUALLY, I THINK THERE *IS* SOMETHING YOU MIGHT BE ABLE TO DO . . .
EH? WHAT ON EARTH HAS RADDY GOT IN MIND?

Fifteen minutes later —
THAT WAS A *BRILLIANT* IDEA, RADDY.
YEAH! GOOD THINKING.

Next day was the children's party —
IT'S GOING REALLY WELL. EVERYONE'S HAVING A GREAT TIME.
EXCEPT MABEL AND VERONICA, THAT IS. BUT THE CHILDREN DON'T REALISE THAT THE SNOBS ARE HATING EVERY MOMENT, SO IT DOESN'T MATTER. ACTUALLY, I THINK THEY LOOK PRETTY COOL IN THESE HATS. HA! HA!

AND NOW WE HAVE A SURPRISE. EVERYONE TO THE MAIN DOOR, PLEASE.

HERE HE COMES — FATHER CHRISTMAS.
OOOH! HE'S GOT *REAL* REINDEER.
THANKS TO *YOU*, RADDY.

NOT REALLY! WHEN I REALISED THE SHERWOODS KEPT SOME REINDEER, IT JUST SEEMED A GOOD IDEA TO USE THEM. AND MR JARVIS MAKES A *GREAT* SANTA!
MERRY CHRISTMAS, EVERYBODY.
THE END

PET
PIN-UP
Bunty

. . . AND THEN HE ASKED ME OUT. I COULD HARDLY BELIEVE IT.
LUCKY YOU, LOUISE. PAUL MARTIN'S REALLY NICE.
YEAH! WISH IT WAS ME!
"The Boy For Me!"
WHERE ARE YOU GOING, THEN?
THE CINEMA — TONIGHT. *OOH,* I CAN HARDLY WAIT.
BRILLIANT. NOW, I HATE TO CHANGE THE SUBJECT, BUT HAVE YOU BROUGHT THAT BOOK YOU PROMISED ME?
OH, NO! SORRY, WENDY, I FORGOT. BUT YOU CAN COME HOME WITH ME AFTER SCHOOL AND PICK IT UP.
OKAY, BUT WON'T YOU NEED ALL YOUR TIME TO GET READY FOR YOUR BIG DATE?
CHEEK! I THINK I CAN SPARE YOU FIVE MINUTES.
So —
HERE WE ARE. HI, BEN.
OH, I DIDN'T KNOW YOU HAD A DOG, LOU.

HE ISN'T *REALLY* OURS. HIS OWNER MOVED ABROAD AND JUST LEFT HIM. HE'S SUPPOSED TO GO TO RESCUE KENNELS BUT THEY'RE FULL, SO WE'RE SORT OF FOSTERING HIM FOR FOUR WEEKS.

I KEEP TRYING TO PERSUADE MUM TO LET US KEEP HIM, BUT HE HASN'T BEEN WELL TRAINED AND HE'S A BIT NAUGHTY SOMETIMES.

A few minutes later, inside —
WHAT A DAY! BEN'S RIPPED A CUSHION AND DUG UP PLANTS IN THE GARDEN. I WON'T BE SORRY WHEN THE FOUR WEEKS ARE UP.
OH, MUM. HE'S JUST HAVING FUN. GIVE HIM A CHANCE. *PLEASE?*

DON'T START THAT AGAIN, LOUISE. HE'S GOING, AND THAT'S THAT!
COME ON, WENDY. WE'LL GET YOUR BOOK.
MUM LOOKS DETERMINED, BUT I'VE *GOT* TO MAKE HER CHANGE HER MIND. I CAN'T BEAR THE THOUGHT OF GIVING BEN AWAY.

Later —
I'M REALLY LOOKING FORWARD TO THIS DATE — BUT I'M NERVOUS, TOO. I HOPE PAUL TURNS UP ON TIME!

He did and, after the movie —
THAT WAS BRILLIANT AND PAUL'S EVEN NICER THAN I THOUGHT. I — I HOPE HE ASKS ME OUT AGAIN.

HOW DO YOU FANCY GOING FOR A PIZZA ON FRIDAY NIGHT? I THOUGHT WE COULD TRY THE NEW PLACE IN THE CENTRE.
OH, YES. THAT'D BE GREAT, PAUL.
THIS IS THE BEST EVENING OF MY LIFE.

The next day —
THE YOUNG
. . . AND THEN WE HELD HANDS. OH, IT WAS GREAT. I JUST WISH IT WAS FRIDAY.
MMM! YOU ENJOYED YOURSELF, THEN?
THIS IS TURNING INTO THE ROMANCE OF THE YEAR.

And —
PAUL'S HERE, DEAD ON TIME AGAIN. I THINK HE'S THE *PERFECT* BOYFRIEND.

But —
HI, LOU . . . OH, NO! A DOG! I DIDN'T KNOW YOU HAD A DOG. KEEP HIM AWAY FROM ME.
IT'S OKAY, PAUL. BEN WON'T HURT YOU.

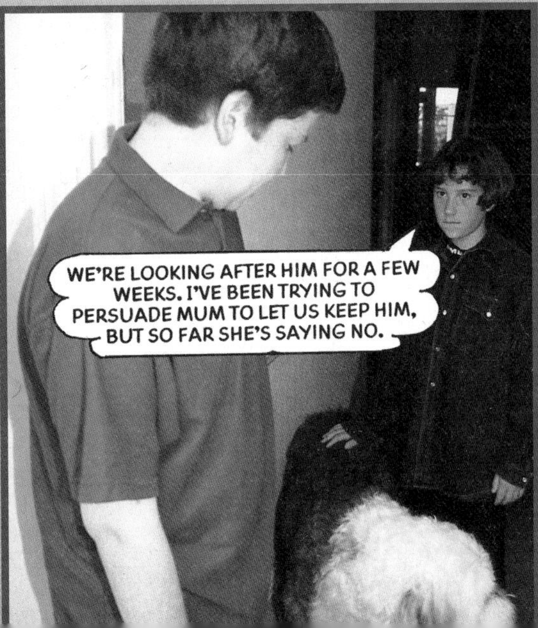
WE'RE LOOKING AFTER HIM FOR A FEW WEEKS. I'VE BEEN TRYING TO PERSUADE MUM TO LET US KEEP HIM, BUT SO FAR SHE'S SAYING NO.

Later —
I'M SURPRISED THAT PAUL DOESN'T LIKE DOGS. MAYBE I'D BETTER FORGET TRYING TO GET MUM TO KEEP BEN. I'LL MISS HIM, BUT IT'LL PROBABLY BE FOR THE BEST IF HE GOES.

Then, on the way out —
HI, LADS. THIS IS MY GIRLFRIEND, LOUISE.
'MY GIRLFRIEND', HE SAID. IT SOUNDS GREAT. THERE'S NO WAY I'M GOING TO RISK LOSING PAUL AS MY BOYFRIEND.

Later —
GOOD BOY. I *WILL* MISS YOU, BEN. BUT I'M SURE YOUR NEW OWNERS WILL LOVE YOU.
I JUST WISH I DIDN'T FEEL LIKE A TRAITOR.

The following week —
COME TO TEA AT YOUR PLACE? YEAH! I'D LOVE THAT, LOUISE. BUT — ER — WHAT ABOUT THAT DOG OF YOURS?
OH, BEN'LL BE OKAY. I'LL MAKE SURE HE BEHAVES.
YOU KNOW, I THINK PAUL'S SCARED OF DOGS, BUT DOESN'T LIKE TO ADMIT IT.

On Sunday —
OH, WHAT'S WRONG WITH THE DOG *NOW?* HE'LL KNOCK SOMETHING OVER IF HE KEEPS THUMPING UP AND DOWN THE STAIRS LIKE THAT.
PAUL'S DUE AT ANY MINUTE. OH, WHY DID BEN HAVE TO CHOOSE *TODAY* TO START BEHAVING LIKE AN IDIOT?

HANG ON! I THINK HE WANTS US TO FOLLOW HIM. SOMETHING'S WRONG.

I WAS RIGHT. BEN MUST HAVE NOTICED THAT THIS PIPE WAS LEAKING. IT'S A GOOD JOB HE WARNED US BEFORE WE HAD A REAL FLOOD. WHAT A CLEVER DOG.
AND TO THINK I CHASED HIM OUTSIDE. I'LL HAVE TO GO OUT AND THANK HIM.

I THINK MUM WOULD BE QUITE HAPPY TO KEEP BEN NOW, BUT I'M NOT GOING TO MENTION IT. I'VE GOT PAUL TO THINK ABOUT.
GOOD BOY, BEN. CLEVER DOG.

Soon —
HERE COMES PAUL. HE LOOKS REALLY SMART, LOUISE.
HE ALWAYS DOES, MUM. I KNOW YOU'LL LIKE HIM WHEN YOU GET A CHANCE TO REALLY GET TO KNOW HIM.

MUM AND DAD, THIS IS PAUL. PAUL, MEET MY PARENTS.
HELLO, MR AND MRS DEXTER.
I THINK MUM AND DAD ARE IMPRESSED.

ARGH! THAT DOG! KEEP HIM AWAY FROM ME.
HERE, BEN. GOOD BOY.
POOR BEN. HE WAS ONLY TRYING TO BE FRIENDLY.

And —
LOOK! HE'S TRYING TO SAY SORRY.
BUT HE'S PUTTING HAIR ON MY TROUSERS. *URGH!*

NOW HE'S PUTTING PAW PRINTS ON MY SHOE. PUSH OFF, WILL YOU?
I'LL GET A DUSTER.
WHAT A FUSS!

A few minutes later —
THAT'S IT . . . *AAARGH!*
I THINK HE CAN SMELL YOUR HAIR-GEL. DOGS' NOSES ARE VERY SENSITIVE, YOU KNOW.

THE WHOLE POINT OF USING GEL IS TO KEEP MY HAIR IN PLACE. NOW YOUR STUPID MUTT HAS MESSED IT UP.
COME ON, BEN. I'LL TAKE YOU OUTSIDE.
PAUL'S DEAD UPSET ABOUT HIS HAIR. I DIDN'T REALISE HE WAS SO VAIN.

Soon —
I'VE ENJOYED MEETING YOUR PARENTS, LOUISE, BUT I *DON'T* LIKE YOUR DOG. I THINK I SHOULD WARN YOU THAT I WON'T BE COMING BACK IF YOU DECIDE TO KEEP *HIM*.
OH, YOU MEAN I HAVE TO CHOOSE BETWEEN YOU?

Next day —
YOU SHOULD HAVE HEARD THE FUSS. ANYWAY, IN THE END HE SAID I HAD TO CHOOSE BETWEEN HIM AND BEN.
WELL, WHICH ONE IS IT GONNA BE?
YEAH! TELL US.
MUM SAID BEN COULD STAY, SO I CHOSE *HIM*. THERE WAS NO CONTEST, REALLY. BEN'S THE BOY FOR ME!
YEAH!
THE END

meet the coolest gang around!

Carly's Crowd!

Hi, guys! Carly Cummings here. My sister, Roz, is at The Comp in snowy Redvale, while I'm living it up here in sunny L.A. Except, I wish *I* was in snowy Redvale, too! The only snow we see here on the West Coast is the fake stuff in the store windows.

"Have you seen the card I got from Dad and Roz?" I asked my buddy, Lori Chomsky.

"Yeah — a zillion times, Carly," Lori sighed. "Gimme a break!"

But I still fetched it for another look. It was one of those cards where they use your own photo — and the photo showed Roz in the snow at Redvale!

"You know, I've been *dreaming* of a white Christmas . . ." I stopped, but it was too late. Lori was already well into song.

"Enough!" I interrupted. "I mean dreaming of Christmas in Redvale with Dad and Roz, and the snow falling and . . ."

"You're getting a snow fixation," Lori grinned.

She's always coming out with stuff like that. Her father's an analyst — you know, a 'shrink'. L.A.'s full of them. Nearly as thick on the ground as plastic surgeons.

One time I said that it would have been better for Lori's family if her dad *had* been a plastic surgeon. It was a joke, right? Only she didn't speak to me for two hours!

But mostly we get on really well, me, Lori, Sammy Tanaka and Marie Gomez. Better sometimes than me and Roz. But Roz is family, you know?

"We're going to the Grand Canyon," Lori was saying to me now. "We're staying in a hotel right over Christmas, and Mom's invited Sammy to come with us. Marie's comin' too — well, after she gets back from visiting her grandad over the border. The whole Gomez gang treks down there every Christmas. Crazy, huh?"

"Not really," I said, clutching my card close. "Christmas *is* a time for family, after all."

"Oh, snap out of it, Carly. Think positively!" Sometimes Lori sounds just like her pop. "Hey! Why not see if your mom'll come with us. She's real close with my mom . . ."

But I never even mentioned it to Mom. I'd gotten it into my head that maybe I'd get to England for Christmas, so I kept hinting — flashing the card and all.

And I kept on hoping — right up until two days before Christmas. Then the bomb dropped.

"I'm looking forward to a quiet Christmas this year, Carly," Mom said to me. "Just you and me. I guess you'll have lots of parties and stuff arranged with Lori and the others, like always."

I smiled. No way could I tell her the truth now.

But I woke up next morning and couldn't keep from crying. Mom must have heard because she came into my room. And then it all came out.

". . . and I got this crazy notion — f-fixation, Lori says — about p-playing in the s-s-snow with Roz!" I was crying again. "It's hard to understand, but . . ." Mom gave me a hug.

"I do understand, honey. Listen, we can't do Redvale — not this year — but we'll see what we *can* do — okay?"

"Okay," I said. I gave her a real smile then, because I got this feeling she really *did* know how I felt.

I heard her on the phone, and soon we were packing stuff into the trunk of the car.

We just drove and drove.

"You going to tell me where we're going?" I asked.

"Nope! You'll have to wait and see." Mom grinned.

We drove on and on, passing mountains and valleys. Then I pointed out the window.

"Hey, Mom, we just crossed the State line!"

"Yep! Welcome to Arizona, Carly!" Mom laughed.

I *knew* where we were heading then.

Soon there was snow all around. Miles of white in every direction.

"Feeling a bit more like Christmas yet?" Mom asked.

"Yeah," I said, smiling.

When we pulled into the parking lot at the hotel, we'd been driving all day. But it was worth it. Lori and Sammy and Marie came rushing out to meet us, followed by Lori's folks. Mom gave Betty Chomsky a huge hug.

On Christmas Day we took a look down at the Grand Canyon, then we played like young kids in the snow. We built a terrific snowman and Mom took a photograph of us all beside him. If it turns out, I'm gonna have it made into a Christmas card to send to Roz next year.

Who knows, maybe I'll be able to deliver it personally but, for now, if I couldn't be with sis at Christmas, there was no-one better than Lori, Marie and Sam.

Have a cool yule, guys!

The New Girls!

PAULA PETERSON was a new scholarship pupil at the famous Dinelli Stage School.
I SEE YOU'VE PUT YOUR NAME DOWN TO AUDITION FOR THE CHRISTMAS PERFORMANCE OF PETER PAN, PAULA.
YEAH! I DON'T SUPPOSE I STAND MUCH CHANCE, BUT I THOUGHT I'D GIVE IT A TRY, ANYWAY.
DINELLI STAGE SCHOOL
QUITE RIGHT. YOU MAY BE NEW, BUT YOU CAN SING — *AND* DANCE! I THINK YOU COULD DO WELL.
THANKS, SAM.
HEAR THAT, KELLI? WE'LL HAVE TO DO SOMETHING ABOUT *THIS!*
WE COULDN'T HELP OVERHEARING WHAT YOU SAID ABOUT THE SCHOOL SHOW, PAULA.
NOW, DON'T TAKE THIS THE WRONG WAY, BUT YOU'RE NOT READY TO AUDITION YET. YOU MIGHT MAKE A FOOL OF YOURSELF.
NEW KIDS USUALLY STAY IN THE BACKGROUND FOR A TERM OR TWO.
BEING PUSHY DOESN'T GET YOU ANYWHERE AT THE DINELLI. WAIT UNTIL YOU'VE LEARNED A BIT MORE BEFORE YOU GO IN FOR AUDITIONS.
OH, I — I DIDN'T REALISE. I'LL TAKE MY NAME OFF THE LIST RIGHT AWAY.
So —
HA! HA! HA! SHE FELL FOR IT! THERE AREN'T MANY DECENT PARTS IN PETER PAN, SO THE LESS COMPETITION WE HAVE, THE BETTER.

Later —
I — I WISH I HADN'T TAKEN MY NAME OFF THE LIST — BUT I CERTAINLY DON'T WANT TO SEEM PUSHY. IT WAS GOOD OF KELLI AND STACEY TO WARN ME.
OH, SORRY! I WASN'T LOOKING WHERE I WAS GOING.
ME NEITHER. I'M NEW HERE, SO CAN YOU SHOW ME WHERE TO REGISTER?
A few minutes later —
THANKS FOR BRINGING ME TO THE OFFICE. I'M NEILA, BY THE WAY. I WASN'T ABLE TO GET HERE FOR THE FIRST DAY OF TERM, SO I'M A BIT NERVOUS.
OFFICE
I'M NEW THIS TERM, TOO, SO MAYBE WE CAN HELP EACH OTHER.
The first lesson was Maths —
NEILA — YOU'RE HOLDING THE PENCIL UPSIDE DOWN.
OH, THANK YOU FOR TELLING ME, PAULA.
And —
DEAR ME, YOU DON'T SEEM TO UNDERSTAND BASIC MATHS, NEILA.
I'M AFRAID THIS SUBJECT WASN'T TAUGHT AT MY LAST SCHOOL.
WE'VE NEVER MET ANYONE SO BACKWARD BEFORE!
CAN'T USE A PENCIL — CAN'T ADD UP! I DON'T THINK YOU'VE EVER *BEEN* TO SCHOOL.
LEAVE HER ALONE. MAYBE NEILA HAS LEARNING DIFFICULTIES.
YEAH — LIKE WE SAID! SHE'S STUPID!

In the dance class, it was a different matter —
WOW! MAYBE KELLI AND STACEY WON'T GO ON ABOUT NEILA SO MUCH NOW. SHE'S CERTAINLY AHEAD OF THE CLASS AT DANCING!
After school —
WHERE DO YOU LIVE, NEILA? ARE YOU GOING MY WAY?
I DON'T THINK SO, PAULA. 'BYE!
BUT I'VE NEVER TOLD YOU . . . OH, SHE'S GONE! SHE MUST HAVE RUN LIKE THE WIND.
Next morning —
I NOTICE OUR CLASS DUMBO HASN'T SHOWN HER FACE TODAY. PROBABLY REALISES SHE'S OUT OF HER DEPTH HERE.
HUH! STACEY AND KELLI ARE A PAIR OF CATS. I WONDER IF I WAS RIGHT TO LISTEN TO THEM EARLIER?
Then —
NEILA — YOU'RE HERE ALREADY.
YES! I CAME ABOUT AN HOUR AGO AND THOUGHT I WOULD START WARMING UP. THE TIME HAS JUST FLOWN BY.
Soon —
PHEW! YOU LOOK AS FRESH AS A DAISY. WHERE DO YOU GET YOUR ENERGY?
I HAVE A VERY LARGE SUPPLY OF THAT, PAULA. UNFORTUNATELY, MY SUPPLY OF EDUCATIONAL KNOWLEDGE IS NOT SO GREAT.

I COULD HELP YOU WITH YOUR READING IF YOU LIKE.
THANK YOU. YOU'RE ALREADY A REAL FRIEND TO ME. IN RETURN, I WILL HELP YOU IN ANY WAY I CAN.
Neila and Paula soon became good friends. Then, a few weeks later —
WHY DO YOU SING SO QUIETLY, PAULA? YOU HAVE A VERY GOOD VOICE.
STACEY AND KELLI WARNED ME ABOUT BEING TOO PUSHY DURING MY FIRST TERM. I WOULDN'T WANT ANYONE TO THINK I WAS SHOWING OFF.
THAT'S RUBBISH! IF YOU ENJOY SINGING, THEN GO FOR IT! I INTEND TO! AFTER ALL, WE ARE HERE BECAUSE WE *LIKE* TO PERFORM.
Then, in the dance class —
YOU DANCE BETTER WHEN OUR TEACHER IS NOT LOOKING. WHY IS THIS?
AFTER WHAT STACEY AND KELLI SAID, I'M WORRIED ABOUT MAKING A FOOL OF MYSELF.
FORGET THEM! THEY WERE ONLY TRYING TO PUT YOU OFF. YOU LOVE TO DANCE, SO ENJOY IT!
I'LL *NEVER* BE AS GOOD AS YOU, NEILA. BUT YOU GIVE ME LOTS OF CONFIDENCE.
Later —
I STILL HAVEN'T CAST ALL THE PARTS IN 'PETER PAN', GIRLS. WOULD YOU TWO LIKE TO AUDITION?
REALLY? WE'D *LOVE* TO, MISS ROSSI.

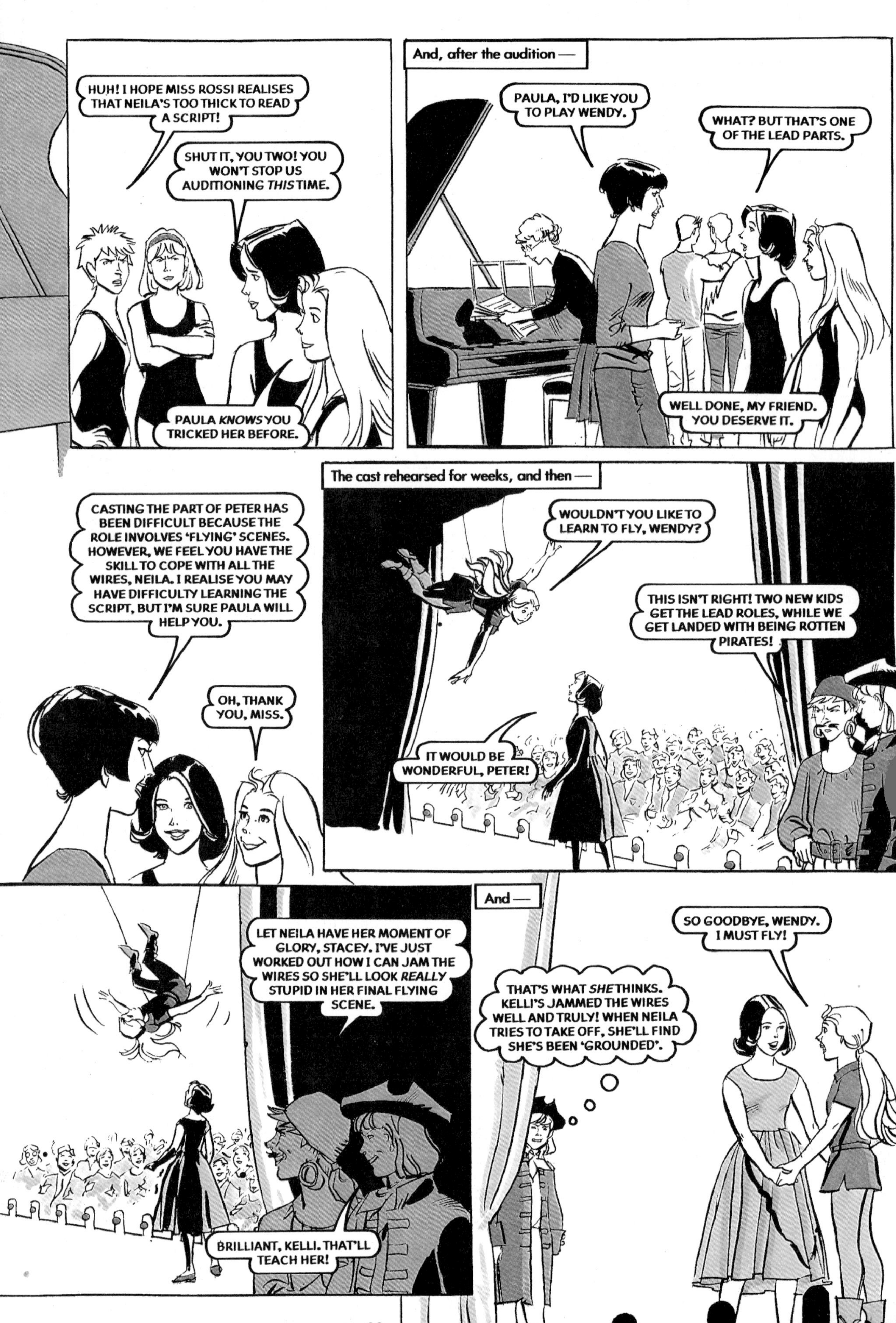
HUH! I HOPE MISS ROSSI REALISES THAT NEILA'S TOO THICK TO READ A SCRIPT!
SHUT IT, YOU TWO! YOU WON'T STOP US AUDITIONING *THIS* TIME.
PAULA *KNOWS* YOU TRICKED HER BEFORE.
And, after the audition —
PAULA, I'D LIKE YOU TO PLAY WENDY.
WHAT? BUT THAT'S ONE OF THE LEAD PARTS.
WELL DONE, MY FRIEND. YOU DESERVE IT.
CASTING THE PART OF PETER HAS BEEN DIFFICULT BECAUSE THE ROLE INVOLVES 'FLYING' SCENES. HOWEVER, WE FEEL YOU HAVE THE SKILL TO COPE WITH ALL THE WIRES, NEILA. I REALISE YOU MAY HAVE DIFFICULTY LEARNING THE SCRIPT, BUT I'M SURE PAULA WILL HELP YOU.
OH, THANK YOU, MISS.
The cast rehearsed for weeks, and then —
WOULDN'T YOU LIKE TO LEARN TO FLY, WENDY?
IT WOULD BE WONDERFUL, PETER!
THIS ISN'T RIGHT! TWO NEW KIDS GET THE LEAD ROLES, WHILE WE GET LANDED WITH BEING ROTTEN PIRATES!
LET NEILA HAVE HER MOMENT OF GLORY, STACEY. I'VE JUST WORKED OUT HOW I CAN JAM THE WIRES SO SHE'LL LOOK *REALLY* STUPID IN HER FINAL FLYING SCENE.
BRILLIANT, KELLI. THAT'LL TEACH HER!
And —
SO GOODBYE, WENDY. I MUST FLY!
THAT'S WHAT *SHE* THINKS. KELLI'S JAMMED THE WIRES WELL AND TRULY! WHEN NEILA TRIES TO TAKE OFF, SHE'LL FIND SHE'S BEEN 'GROUNDED'.

But —
WOW! NEILA'S NEVER GIVEN A DISPLAY QUITE LIKE THIS IN REHEARSALS. SHE'S MOVING SO FAST, I CAN'T EVEN SEE THE WIRES!
I THOUGHT YOU SABOTAGED THE WIRES!
I DID — BUT NEILA WASN'T EVEN *ATTACHED* TO THEM! I TELL YOU, STACEY, SHE WAS REALLY *FLYING!*
I — I JUST CAN'T BELIEVE THIS! WERE YOU TRULY FLYING? BUT HOW?
HAVE YOU STILL NOT WORKED OUT MY SECRET. LET ME GIVE YOU A CLUE! STACEY AND KELLI WERE RIGHT WHEN THEY CALLED ME BACKWARD — CERTAINLY WHEN IT COMES TO MY NAME.
WHAT? NEILA IS A.L.I.E.N.! *ALIEN!* DO YOU MEAN YOU'RE FROM ANOTHER PLANET?
EXACTLY! BUT WE DON'T HAVE STAGE SCHOOLS THERE, SO I CAME TO EARTH TO LEARN TO BE AN ACTRESS.
YOU CERTAINLY TAUGHT STACEY AND KELLI A LESSON TONIGHT!
YES. AND I ENJOYED IT SO MUCH THAT I'M COMING BACK NEXT TERM TO GIVE THEM A FEW *MORE* SURPRISES! SEE YOU THEN, PAULA.
The End

PUZZLE TIME!

CAT TRAP!

C	A	T
C	A	T
C	A	T

Moving from square to square, up, down or diagonally, how many times can you spell the word cat? It's harder than it looks!

Pens at the ready? See if you can solve these animal puzzles

missing links

Solve the clues to complete the word chain. Each letter begins with the last letter of the word before. When you have finished, rearrange the letters in the shaded spaces to find something number 8 might sleep in.

1. Dogs chew on them (5)
2. Horses live in these (7)
3. A male horse (8)
4. _ _ _ _ bags for feeding (4)
5. Where a chicken hatches from (3)
6. A male goose
7. Thumper is one
8. He chases Jerry
9. You'll see one swinging in the zoo
10. The colour of a canary
11. A huge swimming mammal.

SNIFF 'EM OUT!

The following animals are all hidden in our mega word square, but can you find them? They can be read, up, down, forwards backwards or diagonally — so get hunting.

ASS	DONKEY	LION
BADGER	ELEPHANT	OTTER
BAT	FISH	OXEN
BEAR	FOAL	PIG
BUDGIE	FOX	RAT
CAMEL	GIRAFFE	RHINO
CAT	GOAT	TIGER
COW	HAMSTER	WOLF
DOG	HORSE	

B	A	T	T	F	L	O	W	C	T
A	U	W	A	W	O	C	U	B	I
D	R	D	O	G	O	X	E	N	G
G	H	O	G	I	R	A	F	F	E
E	H	N	R	I	R	Z	I	O	R
R	O	K	E	J	E	C	S	A	O
A	R	E	T	S	M	A	H	L	N
C	S	Y	T	G	K	M	T	O	I
A	E	S	O	I	Y	E	I	A	H
T	N	A	H	P	E	L	E	X	R

AND THEY'RE OFF . . .

Quickly, without counting, which donkey passes through the least squares and wins the donkey derby?

MIXED UP MUTTS!

Unscramble the letters below to discover four breeds of dogs.

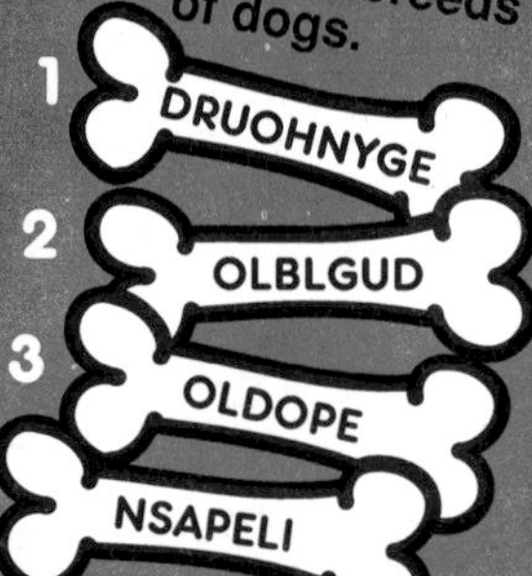

ANSWERS

AND THEY'RE OFF . . .
Daisy passes through **23** squares. **Maisy** passes through **20** squares. **Lazy** passes through **18** squares.
Lazy is the winner

MIXED UP MUTTS!
1. Greyhound, 2. Bulldog, 3. Poodle, 4. Spaniel.

SNIFF 'EM OUT

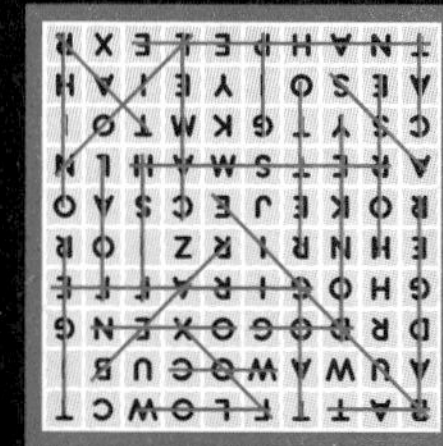

CAT TRAP!
17

MISSING LINKS
1. Bones, 2. Stables, 3. Stallion, 4. Nose, 5. Egg, 6. Gander, 7. Rabbit, 8. Tom, 9. Monkey, 10. Yellow, 11. Whale. The hidden word is basket.

The COMP

IT was the night before Redvale Comp broke up for Christmas and the twins, Hayley and Becky Sinden, had big plans for the next few days —
END OF TERM PARTY TOMORROW, HAYLEY, THEN IT'S OFF TO LAURA'S UNCLE'S FARM AND . . .
OH, NO! TOM'S STARTED YELLING AGAIN!
WHAT'S UP, MUM? IS THERE A PROBLEM?
NOTHING TO WORRY ABOUT, LOVE. HE'LL SETTLE DOWN SOON.
TROUBLE IS, HE'S STARTED *BEN* OFF NOW!
And —
THEY YELLED ALL NIGHT, LAURA. WE DIDN'T GET A WINK OF SLEEP!
NEVER MIND, BECKY. FROM TOMORROW YOU'LL BOTH BE ON THE FARM, AND THE ONLY THING KEEPING YOU AWAKE WILL BE COWS AND CHICKENS AND OWLS AND . . .
OH, THANKS A LOT!
IT WAS DEAD GOOD OF YOUR AUNT AND UNCLE TO INVITE US FOR THE RUN UP TO CHRISTMAS, LAURA.
YEAH! BUT I JUST WISH YOU DIDN'T HAVE TO GO HOME ON CHRISTMAS EVE. CHRISTMAS DAY ON THE FARM IS BRILLIANT.

IS IT TRUE THERE'S TO BE A LIVE BAND THIS AFTERNOON?
OF COURSE! THEY'RE CALLED 'INSIDE OUT'.
NEVER HEARD OF THEM. THEY'RE NOT LOCAL, ARE THEY?
NO. I HEARD THEY COME FROM LONDON.
WOW! ALL THAT WAY FOR A SCHOOL PARTY!
I'VE HEARD THEM PLAY BEFORE, ACTUALLY. THE LEAD SINGER'S CUTE — *AND* HE FANCIED ME. I'M LOOKING FORWARD TO SEEING HIM AGAIN!
IF YOU ASK ME, NO-ONE FANCIES JAYNE THE PAIN MORE THAN SHE FANCIES HERSELF!
QUIET! THERE IS FAR TOO MUCH CHATTER IN HERE. THIS MAY BE THE LAST DAY OF TERM, BUT THAT'S NO EXCUSE FOR NOISE.
GRIM GERTIE'S THE PITS. I'LL BET *SCROOGE* HAD MORE CHRISTMAS SPIRIT THAN HER.
It seemed a long morning but, at last —
THE BAND'S LATE! I THOUGHT EVERYTHING WOULD'VE BEEN SET UP BY NOW.
ME AND FREDDY CAN FILL IN, IF YOU LIKE.
AAGGH! NO, HODGE. HELP!
WE'LL GO HOME FOR OUR GUITARS!
TOO LATE! THE BAND'S HERE! THAT'S THE VAN NOW!
PHEW! SAVED!

Soon —
THESE GUYS ARE WAY COOL!
THEY CERTAINLY SING BETTER THAN HODGE AND FREDDY!
HUH! MY *CAT* SINGS BETTER THAN HODGE AND FREDDY!
JUST LOOK AT THE PAIN BATTING HER EYELASHES AT THE LEAD SINGER!
I THINK YOUR BAND IS JUST GREAT. I'M A BIG, BIG FAN. MAYBE YOU REMEMBER ME FROM YOUR CONCERT LAST MONTH?
I REALLY LIKE YOUR TOP.
YOU DO?
HEY, SOUNDS LIKE HE'S IMPRESSED.
YEAH, MY GIRLFRIEND HAS ONE JUST LIKE IT.
OOPS! WITNESS THE END OF A BEAUTIFUL FRIENDSHIP!
HEY, LOOK — GRIM GERTIE'S COME TO THE PARTY!
I WOULDN'T HAVE THOUGHT THIS MUSIC WAS HER STYLE!

HELLO, RYAN DEAR!
HI, AUNTIE! IT'S GREAT TO SEE YOU!
HE'S HER *NEPHEW!* SO *THAT'S* WHY THIS BAND WAS BOOKED!
YOU HAD A LUCKY ESCAPE THERE, JAYNE. YOU COULD HAVE ENDED UP RELATED TO GERTIE.
HUH!
WOW! LOOK AT *THAT!*
GERTIE'S *DANCING!*
SHE CERTAINLY HAS PLENTY CHRISTMAS SPIRIT NOW!
And, later —
WHAT A PARTY!
SSSH, GIRLS. BEN AND TOM HAVE BOTH COME DOWN WITH CHICKENPOX. I'VE JUST GOT THEM TO SLEEP.
POOR THINGS. NO WONDER THEY WERE FRETFUL LAST NIGHT.
BUT — BUT DOES THIS MEAN WE'RE INFECTIOUS TOO?
WELL, YOU'VE BOTH HAD IT ALREADY, BUT WE'LL HAVE TO RING LAURA'S AUNT AND UNCLE AND TELL *THEM.*
AWW! THEY MIGHT NOT WANT US TO COME NOW.
CHICKENPOX? OH, WE'VE ALL HAD THAT, SO NO PROBLEM.
BRILL!
So, next day —
I THINK MUM WAS QUITE GLAD TO GET SHOT OF US FOR A FEW DAYS. IT GIVES HER PEACE AND QUIET TO LOOK AFTER THE LITTLE ONES.
THIS IS GOING TO BE WICKED. I KNOW IT IS!

And, soon —
HELLO, EVERYONE! MY, YOU TWINS ARE ALIKE. IF YOUR HAIR WASN'T DIFFERENT I'D NEVER KNOW WHICH WAS WHICH.
WELL, I'M BECKY, AND THIS IS HAYLEY. AND WE PROMISE *NOT* TO CHANGE OUR HAIR WHILE WE'RE HERE.
HI, UGLY!
GET OFF, COLIN! HUH! I'D FORGOTTEN ABOUT MY CHARMING LITTLE COUSIN.
YOU MUST ALL BE FAMISHED. I'VE PREPARED A LITTLE SOMETHING TO TIDE YOU OVER UNTIL DINNER!
A *LITTLE* SOMETHING? WOW! I WONDER WHAT *DINNER* WILL BE LIKE.
MMMMM! YOUR COOKING IS WONDERFUL, MRS BRADY!
AUNTIE MAUREEN, DEAR. AND TUCK IN. THERE'S LOTS MORE.
I BET YOUR AUNTIE'S CHRISTMAS DINNER'S SOMETHING SPECIAL!
TOO RIGHT! I'LL TELL YOU *ALL* ABOUT IT WHEN I GET BACK.
For the next three days, the girls had a wonderful time —
GEE UP!
TEA TIME, CHICKENS!
LOOK OUT, BELOW!

WELL, I'LL HAVE TO GO, PATSY. IT'S TIME FOR MY DINNER, TOO.
SOMETHING TELLS ME PATSY ISN'T THE ONLY PIGGY AROUND HERE.
I DON'T WANT TO GO HOME TOMORROW. I COULD STAY HERE FOREVER!
IF YOU STAYED MUCH LONGER, WE'D HAVE TO WIDEN THE DOORS TO GET YOU OUT!
HEY, I THINK IT'S STARTING TO SNOW.
Next morning was Christmas Eve —
YOU WERE RIGHT ABOUT THE SNOW, LAURA. I THINK IT'S GOING TO BE A WHITE CHRISTMAS AFTER ALL.
OH, DEAR. THIS IS TURNING INTO QUITE A BLIZZARD.
THE WEATHER REPORTS SAY THERE'S DRIFTING ON THE ROADS.
I HOPE OUR STEPDAD CAN GET THROUGH OKAY!
But, five minutes later —
THAT WAS YOUR STEPFATHER ON THE PHONE, GIRLS. HE'S CAUGHT IN A SNOWDRIFT JUST TWO MILES FROM HERE.
OH, NO!
DON'T WORRY, MY DEARS. UNCLE JOE WILL TAKE THE TRACTOR AND SNOWPLOUGH AND DIG HIM OUT.
Sure enough —
DAD!
IT'S OBVIOUS NO-ONE'S GOING ANYWHERE FOR A DAY OR TWO, SO IT LOOKS LIKE WE'VE EXTRA GUESTS FOR CHRISTMAS, MAUREEN.
WONDERFUL! THE MORE THE MERRIER!
I'D BETTER RING HOME.

THANKS FOR RINGING, DEAR. WE'LL JUST PUT CHRISTMAS ON HOLD AND CELEBRATE IT WHEN YOU GET BACK. IT'LL GIVE THE BOYS MORE TIME TO RECOVER, ANYWAY.
WE'RE STAYING FOR CHRISTMAS! *YEEES!*
So —
WHO'S FOR MORE PUDDING? AND REMEMBER THERE ARE MINCE PIES AND FRESH CREAM TO FOLLOW.
MMMM!
On Boxing Day —
THEY SAY THINGS ARE MUCH BETTER, SO IF YOU STICK TO THE MAIN ROADS YOU SHOULD GET HOME TODAY.
THANKS FOR EVERYTHING — BOTH OF YOU.
'BYE! THANKS A LOT!
And —
WELCOME HOME, EVERYONE! WE'VE MISSED YOU!
IT'S CHRISTMAS! IT'S CHRISTMAS!
AND WE'VE GOT ALL OUR PRESSIES STILL TO OPEN! BRILLIANT!
Then —
MY SECOND CHRISTMAS HAS BEEN EVEN *BETTER* THAN MY FIRST. BUT I DON'T THINK EVEN *I* COULD MANAGE ANOTHER BITE.
OH, WELL, YOU WON'T BE WANTING THESE, THEN!
ON SECOND THOUGHTS, *NO-ONE* BAKES MINCE PIES LIKE YOU, MUM!
I VOTE FOR TWO CHRISTMASSES *EVERY* YEAR!
The End

FOUR MARYS

FACT FILE

ST ELMO'S
Veritas prevalebit

At last, all the facts on your four favourite schoolgirls.

Full Name: Mary Simpson.
Nickname: Simpy.
School: St Elmo's School for Girls.
House: Bee's.
Previous School: Grove Street School, Ironboro.
Parents: Dad — used to own a grocer's shop but now manages a supermarket.
Mum — Mary Lee was the only one of the Marys' mums who *didn't* attend St Elmo's.
Likes: Going out on her bike, sports, pop music, animals — and being with her special friends.
Dislikes: People (like snobby Mabel and Veronica) making a fuss about her being a scholarship pupil — it makes her feel uncomfortable.
Favourite school subject: Mary enjoys most things but History is her favourite.
Proudest moment: Winning her scholarship to St Elmo's and making friends with the other Marys.

Full Name: Lady Mary Radleigh.
Nickname: Raddy.
School: St Elmo's School for Girls.
House: Bee's.
Previous School: St Kilda's Preparatory.
Parents: Dad — Earl Radleigh of Leahampton, an ex-army Field Marshall who is now Chairman of the Governors at St Elmo's. Mum — Mary Watson, the first ever scholarship girl at St Elmo's.
Likes: Food and being with the other Marys.
Dislikes: People who put on airs and graces (like Mabel Lentham and Veronica Laverly), people mentioning her title, and work — Raddy can be lazy.
Most frightening moment: Raddy was once held hostage in the school by armed robbers.

Full Name: Mary Field.
Nickname: Fieldy.
School: St Elmo's School for Girls.
House: Bee's.
Previous School: Webster's School for Girls.
Parents: Dad and Mum — Mary Jensen, who was once a pupil at St Elmo's.
Likes: All kinds of sports (she's especially good at hockey and running), being with the other Marys.
Dislikes: The snobs — Mabel and Veronica, waiting for things to happen (Fieldy can be impatient and tends to act first and ask questions later.
Ambition: To be an international sports star.
Most exciting moment: When playing hockey, Fieldy once fell against a goal post and knocked herself out. She also played the scarecrow in a school production of The Wizard Of Oz.

Full Name: Mary Cotter.
Nickname: Cotty.
School: St Elmo's School for Girls.
House: Bee's.
Previous School: As a small child Cotty was taught at home so St Elmo's is her first and only school.
Parents: Dad and Mum — Mary Miller, who went to St Elmo's and was best friends with Fieldy's mum.
Likes: Art and music (she has a beautiful singing voice), the other Marys.
Dislikes: Sports — she's not much good at them.
Secret: Cotty used to wear her hair in two very *untrendy* plaits — and that's how she looked when she met Mary Simpson on a train on their very first day at St Elmo's.
Worst moment: Cotty can be a bit of a dreamer — on her first morning at St Elmo's she poured tea into the milk jug.

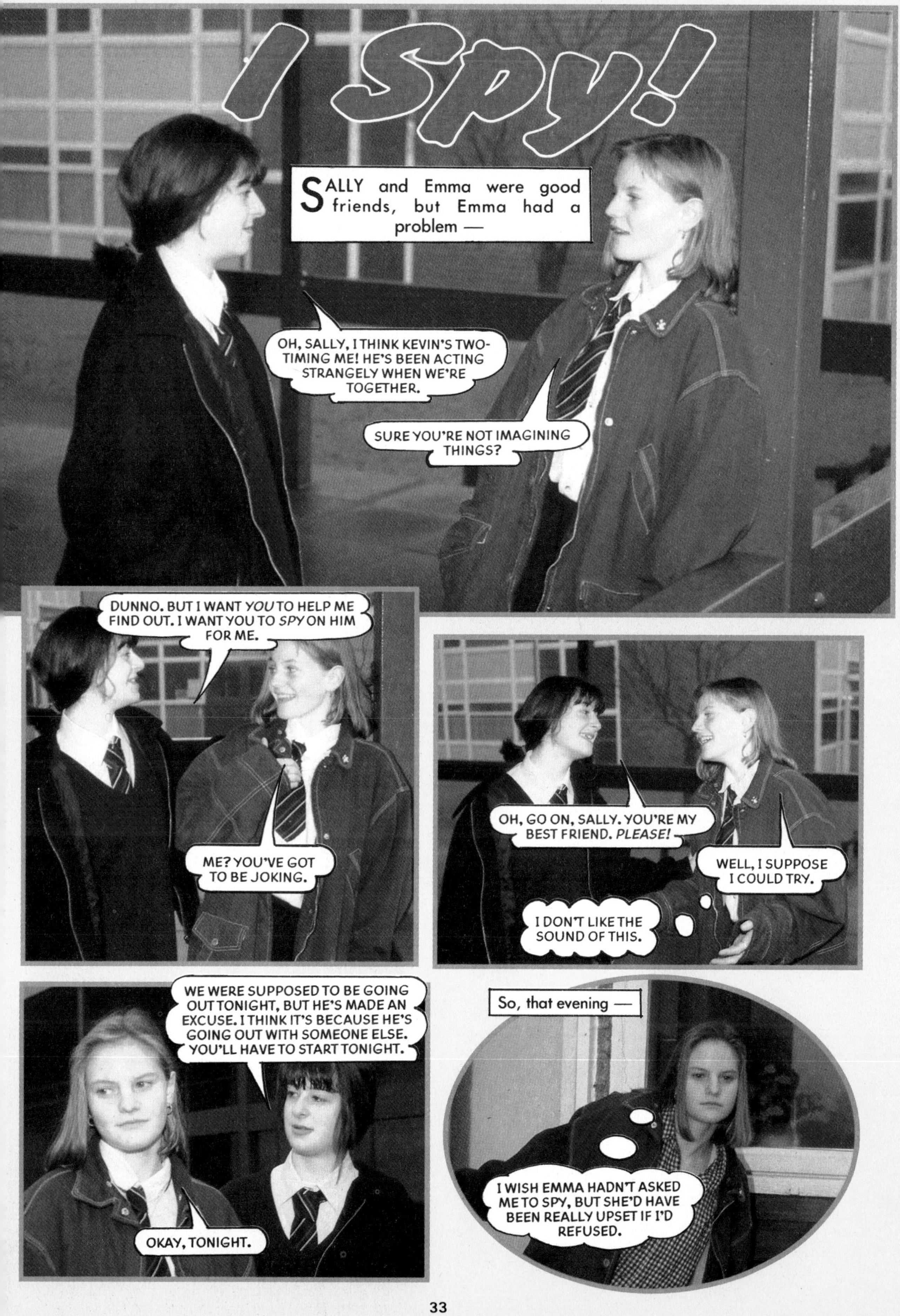

I Spy!

SALLY and Emma were good friends, but Emma had a problem —

OH, SALLY, I THINK KEVIN'S TWO-TIMING ME! HE'S BEEN ACTING STRANGELY WHEN WE'RE TOGETHER.

SURE YOU'RE NOT IMAGINING THINGS?

So, that evening —

Soon —
THERE'S KEVIN, WAITING OUTSIDE THE CINEMA.

And —
HI, KEVIN. I'M HERE!
SALLY! YOU LOOK GREAT! COME ON, WE'RE JUST IN TIME FOR THE FILM.

EMMA WANTS ME TO SPY ON KEVIN, BUT SHE DOESN'T KNOW *I'M* THE GIRL HE'S SECRETLY GOING OUT WITH. I JUST COULDN'T RESIST WHEN HE ASKED ME OUT. AND HE SAYS HE'LL BE FINISHING WITH HER SOON ANYWAY.

Later —
KEV, YOU *ARE* GOING TO FINISH WITH EMMA SOON, AREN'T YOU?
OF COURSE. I'D RATHER GO OUT WITH YOU. BUT I DON'T WANT TO UPSET HER SO I'LL TAKE IT SLOWLY.

Next day —
EMMA'S WAITING TO SEE WHAT I'VE FOUND OUT. I FEEL A BIT GUILTY, BUT IT'S NOT *MY* FAULT KEVIN PREFERS ME.

WELL? HOW DID IT GO?
WELL I FOLLOWED HIM FROM HIS HOUSE, AND I'M SORRY, EMMA, BUT KEVIN *DOES* HAVE ANOTHER GIRL.

I KNEW IT. THE PIG!
SHE LOOKS FURIOUS.

WHAT'S SHE LIKE THEN? IS SHE GOOD LOOKING?
WELL . . . YES, I SUPPOSE YOU COULD SAY SHE'S PRETTY.
I MAY AS WELL BE NICE ABOUT MYSELF.

WHERE DID THEY GO? TELL ME EVERYTHING.
OH, I DIDN'T *FOLLOW* THEM, EMMA. THEY MIGHT'VE NOTICED ME.
THAT'S TRUE, REALLY. I DIDN'T *FOLLOW*. I WAS *THERE*.

HOW *COULD* HE DO THIS TO ME? I'VE GOT TO FIND OUT ALL ABOUT HER — HER NAME, WHERE SHE LIVES, ANYTHING. YOU'LL HELP WON'T YOU, SALLY?
HOW CAN I DO THAT?
SHE'S REALLY ANGRY.

YOU'LL FIND A WAY, SAL. YOU'RE MY BEST FRIEND, REMEMBER?
OH, NOW I FEEL REALLY BAD ABOUT SEEING KEV BEHIND HER BACK. I'LL HAVE TO PRETEND TO HELP UNTIL HE DUMPS HER. I HOPE HE TELLS HER SOON.

ANYWAY, KEVIN AND I ARE GOING OUT TONIGHT, BUT I WON'T LET ON THAT I KNOW YET. I THINK WE'LL GO TO THE CINEMA. IT'S SUPPOSED TO BE A GOOD FILM.
IT IS, BUT HE'S ALREADY SEEN IT. IF SHE ONLY KNEW.

Next morning —
MORNING. HOW DID THE DATE WITH KEVIN GO?
OKAY, I SUPPOSE. HE DIDN'T SUSPECT I KNOW HIS LITTLE SECRET.

YOU WENT TO THE CINEMA THEN, DID YOU?
YEAH. KEVIN SEEMED A BIT BORED, BUT IT WAS A REALLY GOOD FILM. YOU SHOULD GO AND SEE IT, SALLY.

POOR KEVIN. NO WONDER HE WAS BORED, SEEING IT AGAIN SO SOON.

ANYWAY, KEVIN AND ME USUALLY GO BOWLING ON FRIDAY, BUT HE'S CANCELLED. HE *SAYS* HIS GRAN'S VISITING, BUT I SUSPECT HE'S GOING OUT WITH *HER!*
SHE MEANS ME, THOUGH SHE DOESN'T KNOW IT, AND SHE'S RIGHT. KEVIN AND I *ARE* GOING OUT ON FRIDAY.

SO, WHAT ARE *YOU* DOING ON FRIDAY THEN, SALLY?
WHAT?
WHAT DOES SHE MEAN? DOES SHE KNOW?

YOU'RE NOT BUSY, ARE YOU? I WANT YOU TO SPY AGAIN AND GET ME SOME MORE INFO.
OH!
THANK GOODNESS THAT'S ALL SHE MEANT.

ARE YOU SURE IT'S A GOOD IDEA THOUGH, EMMA? I MEAN . . .
COURSE I'M SURE. LOOK, YOU'RE MY BEST FRIEND, AREN'T YOU? SO HELP ME!

Sally had to agree —
THAT GIRL'S GOING TO GET A NASTY SURPRISE WHEN I HAVE MY REVENGE.
WHAT DOES SHE MEAN? WHAT'S SHE PLANNING? AND WHAT AM I GOING TO TELL HER ABOUT THIS OTHER GIRL I'M SUPPOSED TO HAVE SEEN?

On Friday —
. . . AND NOW EMMA KNOWS YOU HAVE ANOTHER GIRLFRIEND.
IT DOESN'T MATTER. WE'RE GOING TO FINISH ANY DAY NOW, AND SHE KNOWS IT.

BUT WE'LL STILL HAVE TO SEE EACH OTHER IN SECRET, THOUGH, KEVIN. SHE'LL BE UPSET IF SHE KNOWS YOU'RE GOING OUT WITH ME.
DON'T WORRY, SHE WON'T FIND OUT.

ANYWAY, I'VE GOT SOMETHING GOOD PLANNED FOR TOMORROW NIGHT. I'VE GOT US FREE TICKETS TO SEE A NEW BAND AT THE EXHIBITION HALL.
BRILLIANT, KEV. THANKS!
IT'LL BE GREAT, AND I'M NOT GOING TO WORRY ABOUT EMMA. I'LL JUST ENJOY MY SATURDAY EVENING.

But, on Saturday evening —
SALLY, EMMA'S HERE. I'M SENDING HER UP.
EH?

DRAT! WHAT'S *SHE* DOING HERE? I DON'T WANT HER TO KNOW I'M GOING OUT. I'LL MESS UP MY HAIR AND PUT THIS OLD TOP ON. I HOPE SHE GOES SOON.

I'VE COME TO TELL YOU KEVIN PHONED ME, AND HE'S DUMPED ME.
OH, EMMA, I'M SORRY.
SHE'S QUITE UPSET. STILL, IT'S FOR THE BEST. I'M GLAD.

WELL, WE CAN HAVE A GOOD GIRLS' NIGHT IN. YOU WEREN'T PLANNING TO GO ANYWHERE, WERE YOU?
ME? ER . . . NO.

WE CAN PLAY SOME OF YOUR TAPES. I WONDER WHAT THAT RAT, KEVIN'S DOING RIGHT NOW?
WAITING FOR ME, I SUPPOSE. OH, WHAT CAN I DO? I CAN'T EVEN GET A MESSAGE TO HIM.

Much later —
I HOPE THIS NEW GIRLFRIEND STOOD HIM UP. WOULDN'T THAT JUST SERVE HIM RIGHT, SAL?
UM . . . YES, I SUPPOSE SO.
HE'LL BE UPSET. I DIDN'T MEET HIM TO GO TO THE CONCERT.

Next morning —
I'VE GOT TO GET ROUND TO KEVIN'S AND EXPLAIN.

But —
I DON'T WANT TO HEAR ANY MORE EXCUSES, SALLY. YOU MADE A FOOL OF ME. WE'RE FINISHED.
FINISHED? OH, I REALLY LIKE KEVIN. WHY WON'T HE BELIEVE IT WASN'T MY FAULT?

On Monday morning —
. . . AND WHEN I SAW THEM TOGETHER IT LOOKED AS IF KEVIN WAS DUMPING HER. HE WAS ANGRY ABOUT SOMETHING. SO . . . ER . . . ARE YOU STILL GOING TO HUNT HER OUT AND GET YOUR REVENGE?
NAH, I WON'T BOTHER NOW.

SERVE HER RIGHT, *WHOEVER* SHE IS. MAYBE *SHE* DIDN'T TURN UP ON SATURDAY NIGHT. MAYBE HE WAITED FOR AGES. WHAT DO *YOU* THINK, SAL?
ER . . . COULD BE.
EMMA LOOKS STRANGE. WHAT'S SHE GETTING AT?

Suddenly Sally realised the awful truth —
YOU *KNOW!* THAT'S WHY YOU CAME ROUND ON SATURDAY NIGHT. YOU'VE KNOWN ALL THE TIME!
YES — BUT I HAD TO MAKE SURE YOU DIDN'T END UP WITH KEVIN FOR YOURSELF. YOU DON'T DESERVE A BOYFRIEND *OR* A BEST FRIEND AFTER WHAT *YOU'VE* DONE.

NOW THAT I'VE DONE THAT *WE'RE* FINISHED TOO, SALLY. I'LL NEVER TALK TO YOU AGAIN.
I'VE LOST MY BEST FRIEND *AND* KEVIN. AND IT'S ALL MY OWN FAULT.
THE END

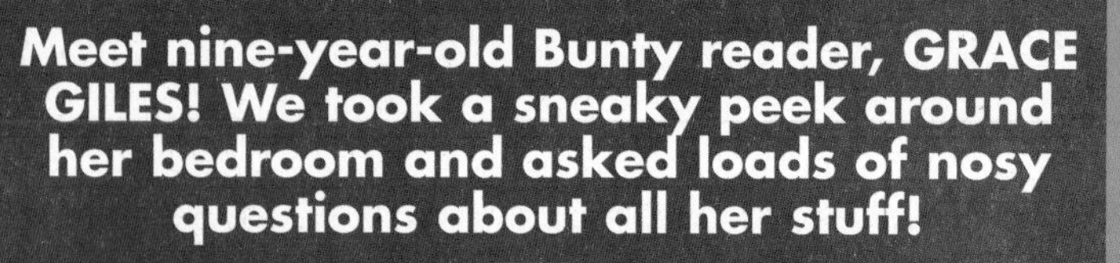

Meet nine-year-old Bunty reader, GRACE GILES! We took a sneaky peek around her bedroom and asked loads of nosy questions about all her stuff!

Do Not Disturb!

I love my clogs! My mum bought them for me in Alnwick where there is a special shop which sells all kinds of dance shoes, and these are specially for traditional clog dancing. I go to clog dancing classes and I'm the only child in the class. I saw my clog dancing teacher dance with her sister at a festival once and decided I wanted to try it!

Burpy Bear is a special bear. He's a special make called a Stieff. Mum's friend brought him back from York for me. When you turn him over he growls, but it sounds a bit like a burp, which is why I called him Burpy!

I have quite a few medals. The ones I'm most proud of are the two for the Great North Run which I have done twice. I've also done the Great North Walk twice. I've got a medal for modern dancing which I did with my friend, Alice, and a medal for playing the fiddle.

The clown puppet was from my friend, Lindsey, and the girl puppet from my grandma for my birthday.

I like Spanish things, especially the postcard with the Spanish dancer on it. The Spanish fan was from my brother when he and my dad went on holiday to Spain. The other fan is from Cyprus.

I keep all my jewellery in this box which my grandma gave me for Christmas — I keep my medals in there too.

My room used to be a bathroom, so I've got a sink, which means I don't have to wait for the bathroom in the morning!

This dress was for my grandma's party. My mum bought it for me, but I went with my mum's cousin, Laura, to buy it. Laura gave me a lovely gold chain to wear with it.

My dad made me this great bunk bed which has a wardrobe underneath for all my clothes. When I was younger I had to share with my brother, Nolan, but now I have a room of my own.

Goosebumps are my favourite books. I have read all the ones in the Rothbury Library and all the ones in the school library. I have some of my own and my brother, Nolan, has some and I've read all of those. They're really scary and sometimes I can't read on, but they don't give me nightmares.

Sandy's Secret
HI, WENDY!
LIKE YOUR JACKET!
NO 'HI, SANDY!' IT'S *ALWAYS* WENDY THE BOYS GO FOR. NOT THAT I'M BOTHERED — THERE'S NO BOYS I LIKE. WELL, EXCEPT MAYBE RICKY AT SCHOOL. HE SEEMS BETTER THAN THE REST.
SANDY and Wendy were good mates, but they had very different personalities.
I'VE GOT A DATE WITH LEON SHARP TONIGHT — NOT THAT *THAT'S* ANYTHING SPECIAL.
DON'T SUPPOSE IT IS FOR YOU — YOU HAVE SO MANY DATES.
I'M TOO SHY FOR BOYS. I'LL CHANGE THE SUBJECT — WENDY NEVER UNDERSTANDS ANYWAY.
ERM — YOU KNOW I LIKE THAT JACKET, TOO.
THANKS! MUM GOT NEIL A NEW TOP SO SHE GOT ME ONE AS WELL.
IT MUST BE HANDY HAVING A YOUNGER BROTHER. MAYBE THAT'S WHY I'M SO SHY WITH BOYS — I'VE ONLY GOT SISTERS.
YOU *MUST* BE JOKING! I'M SURPRISED NEIL AND HIS HORRIBLE MATES HAVEN'T PUT ME OFF BOYS FOR *LIFE!*
I SEE! MAYBE I'M BETTER OFF AS I AM AFTER ALL!
THERE'S RICKY NOW. IT DOESN'T NORMALLY BOTHER ME BEING SHY, BUT I WISH I HAD THE CONFIDENCE TO TALK TO HIM. WENDY WOULD.

Then —
HE'S COMING OVER!
HI, SANDY!

The two got talking, and —
THAT NEW BOWLING PLACE IS GREAT FUN. WOULD YOU LIKE TO COME TONIGHT — WITH ME?
ER — YEAH! I'D LOVE TO.
I DON'T BELIEVE IT!

Later —
IT *WAS* GREAT FUN, LIKE YOU SAID.
RICKY'S SO NICE. BUT I'M NOT AS CHATTY AS WENDY — I HOPE HE WASN'T BORED. I WONDER IF HE'LL ASK ME OUT AGAIN?

BUS TIMES
ARE YOU BUSY TOMORROW AFTERNOON? I PLAY FOOTBALL IN THE MORNING, BUT WE COULD MEET AT OAK PARK GATES ABOUT ONE O'CLOCK.
RIGHT!

The next day, at one o'clock —
THERE HE IS. HEY — WHAT'S HE DOING TALKING TO *WENDY*?

SHE'S GOING NOW. PROBABLY JUST ASKING HIM THE TIME OR SOMETHING, BUT EVEN SO, I DON'T LIKE IT. IF THOSE TWO GET TO KNOW EACH OTHER HE'S BOUND TO PREFER HER — BOYS ALWAYS DO. HE'LL JUST DUMP ME.

Next day —
I PHONED YOU YESTERDAY AND YOUR MUM SAID YOU WERE OUT. WHERE WERE YOU?
OH, NOWHERE EXCITING.
IF I TELL WENDY ABOUT RICKY, SHE'LL BE WANTING US TO GO ON DOUBLE-DATES AND THINGS, AND I DON'T WANT THAT.

YOU SURE?
YEAH — HONESTLY!
I MUST KEEP WENDY AND RICKY APART AND MAKE SURE THEY DON'T GET TO KNOW EACH OTHER BETTER. I COULDN'T BEAR TO LOSE RICKY.

Later, when Sandy met Ricky —
YOU KNOW WE TALKED ABOUT GOING BOWLING AGAIN ON SATURDAY? WELL, IT'S TIM SMITH'S BIRTHDAY AND WE USUALLY ALL GO OUT ON OUR BIRTHDAYS, SO . . .
DON'T WORRY, WE CAN GO BOWLING AGAIN ANOTHER TIME.

On Saturday, Wendy made a surprise visit —
HI! DO YOU FANCY GOING TO THE CINEMA? LEON'S CANCELLED — HE'S GOT 'FLU.
YEAH, I'LL COME WITH YOU.

But, outside the cinema —
OH, NO! THERE'S RICKY! THIS MUST BE WHERE THEY'RE GOING FOR THAT BOY'S BIRTHDAY.

IF THEY SEE US, MAYBE THEY'LL COME OVER HERE, AND RICKY AND WENDY WILL HAVE A CHANCE TO TALK AND HE'LL REALISE HOW MUCH MORE HE LIKES HER THAN ME, AND . . .

OOH, I FEEL *REALLY* ILL. MUST'VE GOT 'FLU, LIKE LEON. IT MUST BE GOING ROUND. I'D BETTER GO HOME.
EH?

AREN'T YOU GOING TO SEE ME HOME? I TOLD YOU, I'M ILL!
BUT YOU CAN GET A BUS RIGHT OVER THERE!

NO, I FEEL ALL FAINT AND WOOZY.
OH, COME ON THEN. WE CAN GO TO THE CINEMA SOME OTHER TIME.

HMM — YOU ARE A BIT HOT.
PHEW! MUST BE 'COS I WAS PANICKING TRYING TO THINK OF A WAY TO KEEP THEM APART.

A few days later —
YOUR GARDEN'S GREAT.
WE CAN SIT OUT HERE IF YOU LIKE. THERE ARE SOME CHAIRS IN THE SHED — YOU GET THEM OUT WHILE I GET US SOME DRINKS.

Then —
WENDY! WHAT ARE *YOU* DOING HERE? YOU DIDN'T PHONE.
I DON'T HAVE TO — DO I? YOU KNOW, YOU'RE ACTING *STRANGE* THESE DAYS.

'COURSE I'M NOT! JUST GO INSIDE. I WON'T BE A MINUTE.

I'LL JUST LOCK RICKY IN THE SHED UNTIL WENDY'S GONE.

Wendy didn't stay long —
SEE YOU TOMORROW, THEN.
SANDY, I KNOW THIS SOUNDS MAD . . .

. . . BUT I KEPT THINKING I HEARD A NOISE LIKE BANGING ON A DOOR. IF IT WAS MY PLACE I'D SWEAR MY BROTHER NEIL HAD LOCKED SOMEONE IN SOMEWHERE. BUT YOUR SISTERS DON'T *DO* THINGS LIKE THAT, DO THEY?
NOT AT ALL. AND THEY'RE OUT, ANYWAY.

When Sandy let Ricky out —
WHAT ARE YOU PLAYING AT? THAT DOOR WAS LOCKED. I WAS BANGING ON IT. DIDN'T YOU HEAR ME?
OH! SORRY, RICKY, I WAS IN THE HOUSE. IT MUST'VE BEEN THE WIND OR SOMETHING.

Next day, at school —
YOU LOOK ROUGH.
I DIDN'T SLEEP WELL.
WORRYING ABOUT KEEPING HER AWAY FROM RICKY!

Later —
I FEEL TERRIBLE.
ARE YOU ALL RIGHT, SANDY?
SHE CAN'T HAVE 'FLU — SHE'S JUST HAD IT.

That evening, Sandy was still unwell —
HI, RICKY. SANDY'S UPSTAIRS IN BED. OH, THERE'S THE DOORBELL AGAIN.
THANKS, I'LL JUST GIVE HER THESE CHOCOLATES.

Sandy had another visitor —
HI, SANDY! BROUGHT YOU SOME GRAPES.
OH, NO, THERE'S *NOTHING* I CAN DO TO STOP THEM GETTING TO KNOW EACH OTHER PROPERLY NOW — NOT WITH ME STUCK IN BED!

But —
RICKY TAYLOR! IF I'D KNOWN *YOU'D* BE HERE, I'D HAVE COME LATER! I THOUGHT THERE WAS EXTRA FOOTBALL PRACTICE TONIGHT ANYWAY.
HANG ON — HOW DO YOU KNOW THAT?

HE'S ONE OF MY BROTHER, NEIL'S, GROTTY MATES, ISN'T HE? *NOW* YOU SEE WHAT I'VE GOT TO PUT UP WITH!
HUH! IF YOU ASK ME IT'S NEIL WHO HAS A LOT TO PUT UP WITH!

SO YOU KNOW EACH OTHER PRETTY WELL?
TOO WELL! *I'LL* COME BACK LATER. AND YOU'RE BETTER OFF WITH *MY* GRAPES THAN HIS MOULDY CHOCS!

SO YOU'RE MATES WITH NEIL'S SISTER, WENDY? AS YOU CAN SEE, WE DON'T REALLY GET ON.
YEAH, I NOTICED! NEVER MIND.
AFTER ALL THAT TROUBLE TRYING TO KEEP THEM APART, THEY DON'T LIKE EACH OTHER ANYWAY!

HEY, YOU LOOK BETTER ALREADY! MUST BE SEEING ME.
MMMM. OR THE CHOCOLATES.
OR KNOWING I'VE NOTHING TO WORRY ABOUT AFTER ALL!
The End

YUMMY!

Make Christmas extra scrummy by rustling up these tasty treats for your friends and family! It's easy!

CHOCOLATE FUDGE — IRRESISTIBLE!

Ingredients

400g granulated sugar
125g butter
125ml milk
100g plain chocolate, broken into pieces
2 tablespoons of thin honey

Utensils

Measuring jug, tablespoon, saucepan, wooden spoon, shallow baking tin, cup, kitchen knife, paper sweet cases.

1. Put sugar, butter, milk, chocolate and honey in the saucepan and heat gently until the sugar has dissolved. Grease the tin.
2. Bring the mixture to the boil, and boil fast for 15 minutes. Don't let it boil over.
3. Test a small amount in a cup of cold water to see if it forms a soft ball. If not, continue boiling until it does.
4. Remove pan and stand on a cool surface for 5 minutes. Beat hard with a wooden spoon.
5. Keep beating until the mixture thickens and feels rough. Scrape it to the edge of the pan and pour into the tin.
6. Leave in a cool place to set. Mark into squares, cut into pieces and put in paper cases. Store in an airtight container.

MINCE PIES — A CHRISTMAS FAVE!

Ingredients

125g plain flour
pinch of salt
50g butter
4 teaspoons cold water
225g mincemeat

Utensils

Sieve, knife, mixing bowl, teaspoon, pastry cutter, pastry brush, cooling rack, rolling pin.

1. Heat oven to 200° C (gas mark 6).
2. Sieve flour and salt into mixing bowl.
3. Cut butter into cubes and rub into flour using fingertips until it looks like fine breadcrumbs.
4. Add water slowly (one teaspoon at a time) whilst mixing with a table knife.
5. Roll pastry into a ball and knead lightly in the mixing bowl.
6. Turn out onto a lightly floured surface or pastry board and roll until ½cm thick.
7. Cut out circles with cutter and place in bun tins.
8. Place a teaspoon of mincemeat into each pastry circle and brush the edges with water.
9. Place another pastry circle on the top of each pie and push the edges together to join them.
10. Brush tops with egg or milk and bake for 10-15 minutes. Remove carefully and place on a cooling rack.

CHRISTMAS TRUFFLES — THE PERFECT GIFT!

Ingredients

100g leftover Madeira cake
1 small orange
25g glace cherries
50g caster sugar
25g ground almonds
4 level tablespoonfuls apricot jam
1 teaspoonful water
chocolate vermicelli (plain and milk varieties)

Utensils

Grater, mixing bowl, chopping board, kitchen knife, palette knife, tablespoon, teaspoon, small saucepan, sieve, wooden spoon, baking sheet, waxed paper, small polythene bag or small bowl, paper sweet cases.

1. Rub cake through fine side of grater. Grate orange rind finely. Put cake crumbs and orange rind into bowl.
2. Finely chop the cherries. Add to the crumbs with sugar and almonds and mix well.
3. Melt apricot jam and water in a small saucepan until runny. Sieve this jam into the cake crumbs.
4. Mix the jam and crumbs until evenly blended and then bind together with the palette knife.
5. Shape mixture into small log shapes in the hands, and stand on a baking sheet covered with waxed paper.
6. Dip truffles into vermicelli until completely coated. Replace on waxed paper and leave to dry. Serve in paper cases.

Always ask permission before using kitchen equipment.

THE SAD SNOWMAN
GEMMA CARSON and her family were moving into their new home, just in time for Christmas.
CAN YOU HELP ME CARRY MY DOLL'S HOUSE, GEMMA?
YES, OF COURSE, CARLY!
CARLY AND DARREN ARE SO EXCITED — AND I FEEL THE SAME. I KNOW WE'RE GOING TO LOVE IT HERE. DAD'S HAD THIS OLD FARMHOUSE MODERNISED AND IT'S TAKEN AGES, BUT WE'RE MOVING IN AT LAST.

MUMMY, CAN WE HAVE A REALLY BIG CHRISTMAS TREE THIS YEAR?
YES! I'VE BEEN THINKING ABOUT THAT, TOO, AND WE'VE CERTAINLY ROOM FOR A BIG TREE IN HERE. IT WOULD LOOK NICE IN THAT CORNER NEAR THE FIRE.
OUR FIRST CHRISTMAS IN OUR NEW HOME! IT'S GOING TO BE BRILLIANT. I JUST CAN'T WAIT FOR CHRISTMAS EVE ON WEDNESDAY!
Early next morning —
HEY — IT'S BEEN SNOWING! BRILL!
GEMMA! COME AND LOOK! THE SNOW'S REALLY DEEP. WE CAN MAKE A SNOWMAN IN THE GARDEN AFTER BREAKFAST, CAN'T WE?
WOW! I CAN'T BELIEVE IT — SNOW FOR CHRISTMAS!
LET'S MAKE A HUGE SNOWMAN, THEN IT'LL LAST *ALL* CHRISTMAS.
OKAY!
THIS IS GREAT! WE DIDN'T HAVE A GARDEN BEFORE, SO WE COULDN'T DO THIS. IT'LL MAKE IT FEEL DEAD CHRISTMASSY HAVING OUR OWN SNOWMAN!
IT'S THE BEST SNOWMAN EVER!
YEAH — HE'S MEGA! WE'LL HAVE TO GIVE HIM A FACE NOW. I'LL GET A CARROT FOR HIS NOSE.
AND WE CAN USE STONES FOR HIS EYES AND MOUTH. HE'S GOING TO LOOK GREAT!
MAKE HIM SMILE, GEMMA. WE WANT A HAPPY SNOWMAN.
THERE! HOW'S THAT? HE'S SMILING NOW.
I'VE GOT DAD'S SCARF! WE CAN USE IT FOR OUR SNOWMAN!
GREAT! NOW — WHAT ABOUT A HAT? I KNOW! THERE'S AN OLD CAP IN THAT SHED AT THE BOTTOM OF THE GARDEN. I SAW IT THERE YESTERDAY WHEN I WAS HAVING A LOOK ROUND.

THIS MUST HAVE BELONGED TO WHOEVER LIVED HERE BEFORE. IT'LL BE JUST RIGHT FOR OUR SNOWMAN.

HOW'S THAT? IS IT OKAY?
YEAH, THAT'S EXCELLENT!
TEA'S READY!

COME ON, GEMMA!

That night —
I KNOW WE'RE GOING TO BE HAPPY HERE. DARREN AND CARLY LOVE IT ALREADY AND SO DO I. WE HAD GREAT FUN MAKING THE SNOWMAN. I HOPE HE HASN'T MELTED BY TOMORROW!

Next morning —
IS OUR SNOWMAN STILL THERE THIS MORNING, CARLY?
YES, BUT COME AND LOOK AT HIM. HIS FACE HAS SLIPPED AND HE LOOKS REALLY SAD AND BAD-TEMPERED.

OH, DEAR! HE *DOES* LOOK GRUMPY! THE SNOW MUST BE SOFT AND THAT'S WHY HIS MOUTH'S SLIPPED. WE CAN'T HAVE HIM LOOKING LIKE THAT AT CHRISTMAS TIME!

OH, DARREN! BE CAREFUL!

OH!
WHAT'S WRONG, SIS?
ER — NOTHING, DARREN. IT'S OKAY.
THAT'S CREEPY! I'M SURE THE SNOWMAN'S FACE CHANGED JUST NOW. BUT THAT'S RIDICULOUS. I MUST HAVE IMAGINED IT.
COME ON, KIDS. TIME FOR TEA.
OUCH!
WHO DID THAT? OH, THERE'S NO-ONE THERE.
WHO CAN HAVE THROWN THAT SNOWBALL? I KNOW IT SOUNDS CRAZY, BUT I'M SURE THERE'S SOMETHING STRANGE ABOUT THAT SNOWMAN!
Later that day —
ARE YOU THE FAMILY WHO'S MOVED INTO THE OLD FARMHOUSE IN LONGMEADOW LANE?
YES, THAT'S RIGHT.

YOU'VE CERTAINLY SMARTENED THE PLACE UP! OLD MR SUTTON, WHO LIVED THERE BEFORE, NEVER SPENT A PENNY ON IT.
HE WAS A REAL OLD SKINFLINT. WE ALL USED TO CALL HIM SCROOGE! HE WOULD SHOUT AND WAVE HIS STICK AT ANYONE WHO WENT NEAR, SO WE JUST LEFT HIM ALONE.
SO THE OLD MAN WHO OWNED THE HOUSE WAS GRUMPY AND BAD-TEMPERED. THAT'S WHAT OUR SNOWMAN LOOKS LIKE WHEN HIS FACE CHANGES.
SO THIS IS WHERE MY BEST SCARF'S GOT TO? LOOK AT IT — NOW IT'S SOAKED THROUGH. WHO SAID YOU CHILDREN COULD TAKE IT?
SORRY, DADDY! WE DIDN'T THINK YOU WOULD MIND.
POOR SNOWMAN! NOW HE LOOKS REALLY SAD. HE'LL BE COLD WITHOUT A SCARF.
LET'S FIND ANOTHER ONE FOR HIM. MUM WILL LET US HAVE ONE OF HERS.
So—
THERE! THAT LOOKS BETTER.
OH, YES! NOW HE'LL BE WARM. MAKE HIM HAPPY AGAIN, GEMMA!
I LOVE YOU, MR SNOWMAN! YOU'RE THE BEST SNOWMAN IN THE WORLD.
THAT'S ODD. I WAS SURE HE WAS LOOKING SAD A MINUTE AGO.
Later that day —
IT'S CHRISTMAS EVE TOMORROW. I WONDER IF IT WILL SNOW AGAIN? OH! WHAT'S THAT? I DON'T BELIEVE IT!

IT LOOKS LIKE THE SNOWMAN'S POINTING! I MUST BE SEEING THINGS! HE CAN'T BE!
Outside —
HE — HE SEEMS NORMAL NOW, BUT I'M SURE THE SNOWMAN WAS POINTING UP AT THE HOUSE.
WHAT WAS HE POINTING AT? OH — WAIT A MINUTE. THERE ARE ONLY TWO ATTIC ROOMS — SO WHAT'S THAT THIRD WINDOW IN THE MIDDLE? IT LOOKS LIKE IT'S BEEN BOARDED UP. I WONDER IF THERE'S A SECRET ROOM UP THERE?
Gemma went to investigate.
I NEVER NOTICED THIS DOOR BEFORE. IT'S LOCKED, BUT THERE ARE SOME KEYS IN THE KITCHEN. MAYBE ONE OF THEM WILL OPEN IT.
THAT'S ODD. I DIDN'T KNOW ABOUT THIS ROOM — I DON'T REMEMBER SEEING IT ON THE PLANS. WHAT'S SO INTERESTING ABOUT IT, GEMMA?
I DON'T KNOW YET! I WONDER WHAT'S IN THAT CUPBOARD?
IT LOOKS LIKE A MONEY BOX. WE'LL TAKE IT DOWNSTAIRS. THERE MAY BE SOMETHING VALUABLE INSIDE.
IT MUST HAVE BELONGED TO THE OLD MAN WHO LIVED HERE. THOSE LADIES SAID HE WAS A MISER, SO MAYBE HE KEPT HIS MONEY HIDDEN UP HERE.

OOH! LOOK AT ALL THE MONEY! THERE MUST BE MILLIONS AND MILLIONS OF POUNDS HERE!
WHAT A HOARD! AND THERE'S A NOTE TUCKED IN HERE.

'TO WHOEVER FINDS THIS: PLEASE GIVE THIS MONEY TO HELP POOR CHILDREN. I HAVE BEEN A SELFISH MAN AND NEVER SPENT A PENNY ON ANYONE ELSE ALL MY LIFE. NOW I'M SORRY FOR MY GREED AND I AM NOT ABLE TO DO ANYTHING ABOUT IT.'

I'LL SPEAK TO THE SOLICITOR TOMORROW. HE'LL KNOW WHAT TO DO ABOUT THIS.
SO IT *IS* MR SCROOGE'S MONEY. HE WANTED THE MONEY TO BE FOUND AND HE USED THE SNOWMAN TO SHOW WHERE IT WAS HIDDEN.

Next day —
THAT'S ALL SETTLED! THERE WAS FIVE THOUSAND POUNDS IN THAT BOX AND IT'S ALL GOING TO A CHILDREN'S CHARITY. LUCKY WE FOUND IT JUST NOW — IT SHOULD MEAN A BETTER CHRISTMAS FOR A LOAD OF KIDS!
GREAT! THAT'S WHAT OLD MR SUTTON WANTED. MAYBE OUR SNOWMAN WON'T LOOK SO GRUMPY AND BAD-TEMPERED ANY MORE.

OH! OUR SNOWMAN'S MELTING! BUT HE'S SMILING! DOES THAT MEAN THE OLD MAN IS HAPPY AT LAST? I HOPE SO! AND MAYBE HE'LL BE PLEASED THAT IT'LL BE A PROPER CHRISTMAS HERE IN HIS HOUSE THIS YEAR. I'VE A FEELING THIS IS GOING TO BE THE BEST CHRISTMAS EVER!
THE END

STAR CH

Just look along the top to find your star sign, and then read do out your star rating for each month to

	Aries (Mar 21 - Apr 20)	Taurus (Apr 21 - May 20)	Gemini (May 21 - June 21)	Cancer (June 22 - July 23)	Leo (July Aug 2
January	Don't be moody! ★	You want to scream! ★★	Hit the sales. ★★★★	A boring month. ★	A friend hel ★★
February	A spooky co-incidence. ★★★	A mystery surprise! ★★★★	All lovey-dovey. ★★★	Rumours and scandal! ★★★	Clean up act ★★
March	A fab surprise! ★★★★	Listen to some good advice. ★★★	Snap out of that dull mood. ★	Running out of cash. ★★★	Choo carefu ★★
April	No time to be shy! ★★★	You'll be extra busy. ★★★	A chance not to be missed. ★★	A new friend. ★★★★	Chang ahea ★★★
May	You'll be seeing red! ★	You have a great idea! ★★★★	Resist telling a fib. ★★★	A dodgy deal! ★★★★	A cha to have ★★
June	A secret message. ★★★★	A new friend. ★★★★	A hot month for romance! ★★★★	Wicked news. ★★	Your lu mont ★★★
July	Don't be stubborn. ★★	Cash, friends and travel! ★★★★	Cash crisis! ★★	Sunshine cheers you up. ★★★	Troub keeping coo ★★
August	Big changes ahead. ★★	Smart new clothes. ★★★	Surprise cash. ★★★★★	Don't be nasty. ★★	You're fe mixed ★
September	Time to pay attention. ★★★	Be careful with cash! ★★	A clean break. ★★	You'll need a favour. ★★★★	Jealou proble ★★★
October	A well-earned rest. ★★★	A mystery guy! ★★★	Some good news. ★★★	A mad month. ★★	Busy Busy ★★
November	Grin and bear it. ★★	A difficult time with friends. ★	Great expectations. ★★	Watch out for gossips. ★★★	Get organis ★★★
December	Surprises and goodies! Lucky you! ★★★★★	Let your hair down! ★★★★	A mega parteee! ★★★	Fun with friends. ★★★★★	Looki good ★★★

way to discover what each month holds for you in 1998! Check e more stars, the better your luck will be!

go g 24 - t 23)	Libra (Sept 24 - Oct 23)	Scorpio (Oct 24 - Nov 22)	Sagittarius (Nov 23 - Dec 22)	Capricorn (Dec 23 - Jan 20)	Aquarius (Jan 21 - Feb 19)	Pisces (Feb 20 - March 20)
fresh tart. ★★	A groovy idea. ★★★★	You're in a whirl. ★★★	Your waiting pays off. ★★★	Lazy month. ★★★	You're in a mood! ★★★	A new friend. ★★
s! You ake a nder. ★★	The truth will hurt. ★★★	Things settle down. ★	A dilemma to think about. ★★★★	Trouble ahead! ★	Music gets you smiling. ★★	You cause a stir. ★★★
new bby? ★★	Say how you feel. ★★	A mystery. ★★★	Someone's playing games. ★★★★	You save the day. ★★★	Feelin' good! ★★★★	You're on top form. ★
ring in r step. ★★★	Lookin' good. ★	A mega bust -up. ★★	You go all sloppy! ★★★	A plan goes wrong. ★★	Give as good as you get! ★★★	It's your lucky month. ★★★★★
r lucky onth. ★★★	A new friend. ★★	Don't miss a chance. ★★★★	You're lookin' good! ★★★★	Cash crisis. ★★★	More problems! ★★★	You blow your top! ★
iends ke you mile. ★★	Secrets to keep. ★★★	You're in hot water. ★★★	Don't overdo it! ★★	Fun, fun, fun! ★★★★★	Havin' fun. ★★	A mellow month. ★★★★
o for it! ★★	Your lucky month. ★★★★★	Holiday fun. ★★	You could lose your temper. ★	Working hard. ★★★	Everything's cool! ★★★	Cash crisis. ★★
roblems r you. ★★	You'll get noticed! ★★★	Your lucky month. ★★★★★	A friend needs help. ★★	Taking a break. ★★★	A hot date. ★★★★★	A new look. ★★★
on't take isks. ★	Nervous? Don't be! ★★★★	Be confident! ★★★	A new look for you. ★★★★★	A great idea. ★★	Delicious gossip! ★★★★	A groovy idea ★★
plan ks well. ★★★	Smiles all round. ★★★	Stick to your guns. ★★	Plenty fun. ★★★	You take a chance ★★	Jealousy problems. ★★★	A plan works well. ★★★★
ou're on form. ★★★	Stay out of trouble. ★★	You need to explain. ★★★	Takin' it easy. ★★★★	Friends surprise you. ★★★	You're in the right! ★	A boring month. ★★★
exciting onth. ★★★	A mega surprise! ★★★★	A perfect ending. ★★★	Mad month! ★★★	Non-stop parteee! ★★★★	Crazy fun! ★★★	A super surprise. ★★★★

BEST FRIENDS'

Having a best friend is COOL! Meet 2 sets of Bunty best friends and read all about them! Plus a guide to being the BEST, best friend!

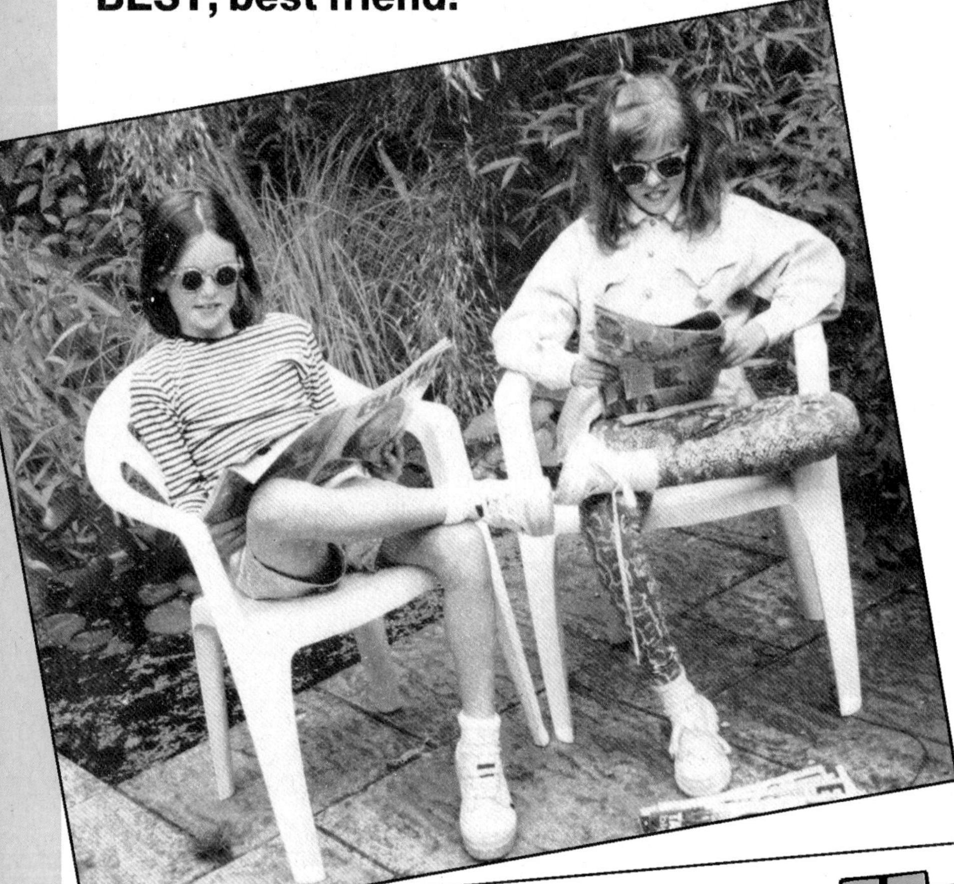

Emily and Sarah

Live: Southampton
Met: At school
Best Friends for: Three years
Emily on Sarah: "She's funny."
Sarah on Emily: "She's nice and kind."
Do they argue: Very rare
Same hobbies: Yes
Best friends should . . . listen to your problems
Ambitions: Emily — teacher or actor
Sarah — author, teacher, actor, work with animals, waitress, work in a shop
Nicknames: Elimy and Cassy
Like boys: No
Fave Film: Mrs Doubtfir
Fave TV: EastEnders an Neighbours
Fave band: Eternal

ARE YOU THE BEST

Answer these questions to reveal the truth!

1. ***Your best friend tries on an outfit which makes her look awful! Do you . . .***
   a . . . *say* it looks awful?
   b . . . suggest some other style?
   d . . . say it looks okay (you don't want to upset her)?
   c . . . say it's up to her?

2. ***You don't like your best friend's boyfriend. Do you . . .***
   a . . . tell her to choose — it's him or you?
   c . . . try to put her off him?
   b . . . let her make up her own mind?
   d . . . pretend you *do* like him?

3. ***Your best friend is feeling down in the dumps. What do you do?***
   c . . . tell her to cheer up
   d . . . anything you can think of to cheer her up
   b . . . ask what's wrong
   a . . . leave her alone

4. ***Your best friend falls flat on her face in front o the whole class at school. You . . .***
   c . . . laugh uncontrollably
   b . . . help her up and have a giggle about it later (when her red face has gone away)
   d . . . rush to see if she's okay
   a . . . run away

5. ***You get a new CD and you know your best fri has wanted it for ages. Do you . . .***
   d . . . let her borrow it immediately?

SPECIAL

la and Louise
ve: Stonehaven
et: At school
est Friends for: Six
ears
la on Louise: "She
akes me laugh, listens to
e and is fun to be with."
ouise On Isla: "She
ometimes teases me
bout boys but we don't
gue. She's helpful and
n."
o they argue: Not really
ame Hobbies: Yes,
ighland Dancing,
llerblading, swimming,
ading
est Friends should . . .
e fun, understanding and
ustworthy, help with
oblems
mbitions: Isla — to be a
shion designer and own
big company
ouise — to make clothes
nd jewellery
icknames: La La (Isla)
nd Lou Lou
Like Boys: Yes, but some
are annoying pests!
Fave Film: Forrest Gump
Fave TV: Sister Sister,
Neighbours and Home
and Away
Fave group and singer:
Boyzone and Peter Andre

FRIEND?

b . . . let her borrow it after you've listened to it?
c . . . let her hear it at your house?
a . . . hide it so she can't borrow it?

Best Friends Do . . .
. . . make you laugh
. . . tell you the truth
. . . stand by you
. . . help you with your problems
. . . listen to you
. . . give you confidence
. . . keep your secrets safe

Best Friends Don't . . .
. . . gossip about you
. . . let you down
. . . steal your boyfriend!
. . . ignore you
. . . go off with someone else
. . . tell you lies
. . . tell your secrets

CONCLUSIONS

Mostly As
You can be very selfish!

Mostly Bs
You could be the perfect best friend.

Mostly Cs
You could show a bit more concern for your best frien

Mostly Ds
You're sometimes too soft and need to stick up for
yourself more.

Hayley's Holiday

HAYLEY WATT and her mates were pupils at Colwich Comprehensive School. One day —

NOTICE BOARD

SKIING TRIP

LOOK! THERE'S GOING TO BE A SCHOOL SKI TRIP IN JANUARY. LET'S PUT OUR NAMES DOWN.

GREAT IDEA!

WHAT ABOUT YOU, HAYLEY?
I DON'T FANCY IT. I LIKE TO GO SOMEWHERE HOT FOR MY HOLIDAYS, AND LIE BESIDE A POOL. ANYWAY, I CAN'T SKI.

YOU'LL LEARN. IT'S EASY — AND SKIING'S FUN! YOU'LL ENJOY IT WHEN YOU TRY.
GO ON! WE'RE ALL GOING.
OH — ALL RIGHT THEN.

So, a few months later —
HERE WE ARE! THE ALPS!
BRR! IT LOOKS COLD!
MAYBE, BUT YOU CAN GET SUN TANNED ON THE SLOPES.

The next day —
I LIKE YOUR DESIGNER SUNGLASSES, LIZZIE!
WANT TO BORROW MY SUN BLOCK, HAYLEY?

NO THANKS! I'M KEEPING MY SCARF ON. IT'S *FREEZING!*
COME ON! YOU WON'T HAVE ANY FUN LIKE THAT.

On the slopes —
NOW I'M GOING TO TEACH YOU HOW TO TURN. WE'LL DO A 'SNOW-PLOUGH', BY POINTING THE TIPS OF OUR SKIS TOGETHER . . .

EASY-PEASY!
AAH!

UP YOU GET.
IT'S NO GOOD. I CAN'T GET THE HANG OF IT.

Later —
CAREFUL, HAYLEY!
HELP!

Several falls later —
I'M BLACK AND BLUE! I'M NOT ENJOYING THIS AT ALL. I DON'T HAVE A GOOD ENOUGH SENSE OF BALANCE FOR SKIING.
The following day —
WE'RE GOING TO TRY A MORE DIFFICULT SLOPE TODAY. ARE YOU COMING, HAYLEY?
NO THANKS!
I CAN'T EVEN MANAGE THE NURSERY SLOPES, SO I'M NOT GOING ANYWHERE HARDER.
I'LL JUST HAVE TO STAY ON THIS NURSERY SLOPE ON MY OWN, WHILE MY MATES HAVE FUN HIGHER UP. WHAT A DRAG! I REALLY WISH I HADN'T COME ON THIS HOLIDAY.
HURRY UP! YOU'RE HOLDING PEOPLE UP.
SORRY!
I'D BETTER START, I SUPPOSE.
MAYBE I'LL BE BETTER TODAY, WITHOUT MY MATES AROUND TO DISTRACT ME.
But —
I'M NOT! I'M OUT OF CONTROL AGAIN!
WATCH OUT!
AAH!
OOF!

I'M REALLY SORRY. I'M HOPELESS.
ME, TOO. I CAN'T MASTER THESE SKIS AT ALL.

OH, DEAR! I THINK I'VE HURT MY WRIST.
OUCH! AND I'VE TWISTED MY ANKLE.

ck at the hotel where Hayley and arl's groups were both staying —
NEITHER OF YOU IS SERIOUSLY HURT, BUT YOU'LL BOTH NEED TO REST A BIT. NO MORE SKIING THIS HOLIDAY, I'M AFRAID.
I DON'T MIND! I WASN'T ENJOYING IT ANYWAY.
NOR WAS I. IT'LL BE LONELY WITHOUT MY MATES, THOUGH.

YES, IT WILL.
UNLESS . . . SUPPOSE WE SPEND OUR TIME TOGETHER?
THAT'S A GREAT IDEA! CARL'S NICE.

ANOTHER COLA BEFORE WE HAVE A DIP IN THE POOL, HAYLEY?
THANKS, CARL.

GREAT! THIS IS JUST THE KIND OF HOLIDAY I WANTED IN THE FIRST PLACE!
THE END

GOING PLACES

"I DON'T want to go," cried Wanda, flinging her bag on the floor. Mum had given her the news as soon as she came in from school, and it was terrible news.

"But it's only for a year," said her mum. "We ought to be proud of Dad, being chosen to start up the company's new office. There were a lot of others after the job, you know."

"But I don't want to leave my friends," she complained. "I won't fit in at this new place. You don't know what it's like, Mum. They'll make fun of my name and my hairstyle and . . . oh, everything."

She could just picture them now, all staring and saying, "Have you seen the new girl?" They'd ask lots of questions and nudge and smile. She remembered when Jenny Smith joined their class last term. Everybody was interested in her, but at least Jenny's name wasn't so very different from everyone else's.

"Can't we stay here, Mum?" she pleaded.

Mum stood up.

"You'll have to get used to the idea, Wanda," she said sternly. "We're going and that's that."

Wanda lay awake for a long time that night, worrying. When she finally slept she dreamed of being surrounded by the girls at her new school, all curious about her and poking fun. In the morning she knew it was only a dream, but it made her feel worse.

At school she told her classmates.

"It'll be really exciting," said Rosie. "Lucky you!"

"Lucky?" shrieked Wanda. "You've got to be joking."

She glared at Rosie. What does she know about anything, she thought.

"We'll miss you, Wanda," said Clare, and the rest agreed.

"Not as much as I'll miss you," she replied. She was having trouble keeping back the tears by now, but they couldn't believe she was so upset about going. They all agreed with Rosie.

"It's only for a year, though, Wanda," said Clare. "I mean, it's not as if we'll never see you again, is it?"

Wanda sniffed. Clare had a point there, though she supposed everything would be different when she got back.

Everything seemed to happen very quickly after that. Packing cases appeared and were filled and Wanda found herself busy, with little time for worrying. But soon it was her last day at school.

"See you next year, Wanda."

"Have a good time."

"Send us a postcard," called Clare, and everyone laughed at that.

Wanda smiled, too. She knew she would not be sending any postcards.

It was a long journey. Mum and Dad were full of enthusiasm and really looking forward to everything. Wanda kept her nose in her book most of the time, and eventually she fell asleep.

"Wanda, we're here." She woke up to find Mum was gently shaking her shoulder. She stood on her own, looking round sleepily while Mum and Dad were hiring a vehicle to drive to their new house.

All she could think was that she wanted this year to be over so she could go back home. She just knew she wouldn't like anything.

But she couldn't help liking their house. It was so bright and spacious, and she loved her bedroom. It had fitted wardrobes and a shower cabinet, but best of all it had a fitted computer station. She cheered up just a little as she thought of getting new games, some she'd never played before.

Next day, though, the knot was back in her stomach. She was going to school.

It was just as she had imagined. Everybody was interested in her.

"Tell us your name," said one, who Wanda thought was probably the captain.

Here we go, she thought. "Wanda."

"Wanda," repeated the girl slowly. She saw them all whispering it, passing it round. She knew they would think it sounded strange.

Questions came thick and fast all morning and she did her best to answer them. They wanted to know about her old school.

"Homework?" they cried, when she mentioned it. "How terrible!"

She was pleased to learn they were never given any. A year without homework! This new school wasn't too bad. She realised she was an object of interest but at least everybody was friendly.

The school itself was amazing. They had computers in every classroom.

"What are you going to have for lunch?" asked the girls at the end of the morning.

"I'll see what there is first," she replied. How did they expect her to choose before they were even in the dining room? She hoped the food was good.

To her surprise the girls explained she could have what she liked. It was just a matter of ordering it through the computer, using her own special number they got for her from the school office. They all laughed at her astonishment and crowded round to see what she would order. Nothing extravagant, she thought. She would save those ideas for another day. So, she ordered pizza and baked beans, but went a little wild on the dessert. She chose toffee ice cream with a caramel sauce, and strawberries. Some of the other girls thought that sounded nice, so they ordered it too.

When she arrived home that afternoon, Mum was waiting and Wanda could see she looked rather anxious.

"Well, how was it, love?"

"Great, Mum. I've had a good day."

"Really?" Mum smiled. "There, I told you it would be all right."

And it would. Wanda knew that now. There were so many things to look forward to. Spending a year on the planet Zelcor was going to be fun, after all.

THE END

FIONA'S FRIEND
FOURTEEN-YEAR-OLD Lisa Jones had agreed to look after seven-year-old Fiona Lee while their mums had a day out.
ARE YOU SURE YOU'LL BE OKAY LOOKING AFTER LITTLE FIONA FOR THE DAY, LISA?
'COURSE I WILL, MUM. STOP WORRYING AND ENJOY YOUR DAY OUT WITH YOUR FRIEND.

MARION AND I HAVE BEEN LOOKING FORWARD TO THIS FOR AGES, BUT SHE COULDN'T HAVE GONE IF YOU HADN'T OFFERED TO LOOK AFTER FIONA.
I KNOW. NOW GO AND HAVE A GREAT TIME. FIONA'S A NICE KID, SO THIS SHOULDN'T BE TOO DIFFICULT.

THAT'S MARION NOW. 'BYE, LISA!
'BYE, MUM! HAVE A NICE DAY!

Then —
HI, FIONA!
HELLO, LISA. I'VE BROUGHT MY FRIEND, TAMMY, WITH ME. IS THAT OKAY?

OH! ER . . . YES, OF COURSE. HELLO, TAMMY.
IT'S A BIT MUCH EXPECTING ME TO LOOK AFTER *TWO* LITTLE GIRLS WITHOUT MENTIONING IT FIRST, BUT I SUPPOSE THEY CAN PLAY TOGETHER.

WELL, WHAT SHALL WE DO FIRST?
WE WANT TO DO SOME COLOURING, PLEASE.

OKAY! DO YOU LIKE COLOURING, TAMMY?
YES, SHE DOES.

So —
IT'S LUCKY I GOT TWO COLOURING BOOKS THE SAME ON SPECIAL OFFER. THEY CAN SHARE THE CRAYONS.
HERE YOU ARE — ONE FOR YOU, FIONA, AND ONE FOR YOU, TAMMY.
COLOURING BOOK

Soon —
YES, TAMMY *ALWAYS* DOES THE SAME AS ME.
THEY'RE NICE, GIRLS. YOU'RE DOING THEM EXACTLY THE SAME.

DO YOU WANT SOMETHING TO DRINK? THERE'S BLACKCURRANT OR ORANGE JUICE, AND CHOCOLATE BISCUITS OR GINGER SNAPS.
WE'LL BOTH HAVE ORANGE AND CHOCOLATE BISCUITS, PLEASE.

But —
TAMMY'S NOT HAVING ANYTHING, AND SHE HASN'T SAID A WORD SO FAR. I DON'T THINK SHE'S VERY HAPPY HERE. AFTER ALL, SHE DOESN'T KNOW ME.

Soon —
HOW ABOUT PLAYING OUT IN THE GARDEN?
OOH, YES! I'M GOOD AT SKIPPING. TAMMY IS AS WELL.

So —
LOOK AT ME, LISA. I CAN SKIP FOR AGES! TAMMY CAN, TOO.
IT LOOKS LIKE TAMMY *ALWAYS* DOES WHAT FIONA DOES.

Soon —
THERE ARE CARTOONS ON TELEVISION IN A FEW MINUTES. I BET YOU LIKE CARTOONS, DON'T YOU?
YES, WE BOTH DO.

I WISH FIONA WOULD LET TAMMY ANSWER FOR HERSELF.
SO YOU LIKE WATCHING CARTOONS, THEN, TAMMY?
'COURSE SHE DOES! COME ON, TAMMY!

A few minutes later —
I'M WORRIED ABOUT TAMMY. I DON'T THINK SHE'S ENJOYING HERSELF. STILL, MAYBE SHE'LL LIKE HER LUNCH.
HA! HA! LOOK AT THAT!

At lunch —
DON'T YOU LIKE YOUR LUNCH, TAMMY? OH, THERE'S THE PHONE!
SHE'S NOT HUNGRY, LISA.

OH, YOU'VE EATEN SOME, TAMMY. THAT'S GOOD!
ALTHOUGH FROM THE LOOK ON FIONA'S FACE I THINK MAYBE *SHE'S* EATEN IT.

AFTER I'VE WASHED UP, I THINK WE'LL GO TO THE PARK.
HOORAY! I *LOVE* GOING TO THE PARK! TAMMY DOES, TOO.

Soon —
TAMMY STILL HASN'T SAID A WORD TO ME, BUT I SUPPOSE SHE MUST TALK TO FIONA OR THEY WOULDN'T BE FRIENDS.

THAT LOT SHOULDN'T BE COMING TO THE SWINGS. THEY'RE TOO BIG FOR THEM.
PUSH ME HIGHER, LISA! AND TAMMY, TOO!

I THINK I'LL TAKE TAMMY AND FIONA AWAY FROM HERE.

LET'S GO ON THE ROUNDABOUT NOW.
THE SOONER I GET THEM AWAY FROM THOSE BOYS, THE BETTER!

A few moments later —

FIONA! MOVE!

THAT SWING CAN'T STOP AND IT'S GOING TO HIT HER!

OH! TAMMY'S PULLED HER OUT OF THE WAY — JUST IN TIME!

IF FIONA HAD BEEN HIT BY THAT SWING, SHE COULD HAVE BEEN REALLY BADLY INJURED. WELL DONE, TAMMY. YOU SAVED HER, JUST IN TIME.

I FEEL REALLY BAD NOW — MUMPING ABOUT HAVING TO LOOK AFTER TAMMY. I'M SO GRATEFUL SHE WAS HERE TO SAVE FIONA.

Later —
THEY'VE BEEN VERY QUIET SINCE WE CAME BACK — PLAYING WITH MY OLD DOLLS. AH, I THINK I CAN HEAR MUM AND MARION.

Soon —
THANK YOU FOR LOOKING AFTER FIONA, LISA. I'M REALLY GRATEFUL.
MUMMY!

BUT WHAT ABOUT TAMMY, FIONA? WHERE IS SHE?
OH, NO! NOT TAMMY *AGAIN!* WE'VE HAD A LOT OF PROBLEMS WITH HER.

WELL, *I'VE* BEEN A BIT CONCERNED ABOUT HER, TOO.
FIONA HAS PLENTY OF FRIENDS. THERE'S NO NEED TO HAVE THIS PRETEND FRIEND ANY MORE.

PRETEND FRIEND?
SO TAMMY'S ONLY A *PRETEND* FRIEND? THAT'S WHY SHE'S DISAPPEARED. BUT — BUT I *SAW* HER!

TAMMY MAY BE ONLY A PRETEND FRIEND, BUT SHE SAVED FIONA TODAY. SHE REALLY *IS* FIONA'S FRIEND.
The End

So you want to party? We've all the info you need to make it perfect!

WHY HAVE A PARTY?

To celebrate! It's your birthday, the end of school or an anniversary.
For fun! Hallowe'en, Bonfire Night and Christmas are all excellent times to hold a party.
To surprise someone! It's their birthday, they're leaving home, coming back or have done well in an exam.
To cheer someone up! Whatever's up, make them smile.
Because you WANT to! There doesn't have to be a reason.

WHAT WILL YOU EAT AND DRINK?

All the fab food on page 48. Check it out! Plus . . . cake, crisps, nuts, pizza, sausage rolls, potato wedges, sweets, ice-cream, jelly, savouries — you name it!
Drinks? Cola, lemonade, fruit and sparkling mineral water, ice-cream floats, milkshakes, fruit punch. Yum!

WHO WILL YOU INVITE?

All your favourite people Friends, family, boys. Send out invitations a few weeks in advance and match them to your party! Write the details on balloons or make invitations a strange shape or colour.

WHERE SHOULD YOU HOLD IT?

Your home? This is fine for slumber or family parties, but be careful not to make too much noise or mess.
A hall or youth club? Great for lots of folk who want to dance.
Burger bar or pizza place? It's all organised for you and you know the food will be yummy!
Your garden? Superb on a sunny day and brill on Bonfire Night.

WHAT WILL YOU WEAR?

Your favourite outfit? You'll know you look great!
Something pink? Or purple, or orange or green? A clown costume? Unless it's not fancy dress!
Pyjamas? In case you decide to slumber.

WILL YOU PLAY GAMES?

Pass The Parcel and Musical Chairs may sound a bit naff, but they'll make everyone join in and have fun. What else can you think of?

WANT TO TRY SOMETHING DIFFERENT?

Fancy dress? Look great and have a laugh!
Colour? In the pink or feeling blue? You decide! (Make food and decor match, too!)
Slumber? Scoff yourself silly then stay awake all night . . . or sleep it off.
Disco? Grab your mates and party!

HOW ABOUT MUSIC?

Buy — CD or cassette compilations. A whole range of party sounds.
Borrow — ask friends and family if you can borrow their music, or make up a tape of your own faves.
Karaoke — music and fun — all in one!

WILL YOU ENJOY YOURSELF?

You bet!

SADIE'S SUMMER
TWELVE-YEAR-OLD Sadie Waters was the youngest maid in Mr and Mrs Parker-Smythe's Victorian household. One hot day in July, Sadie was hard at work as usual —
STOP SLACKING, GIRL! THERE'S A LOAD MORE WASHING STILL TO BE DONE.
IT'S SO HOT IN HERE, MRS GRIGGS. I FEEL FAINT. CAN'T I SIT DOWN FOR A SECOND?

CERTAINLY NOT! YOU'RE HERE TO WORK. AND WHEN YOU'VE FINISHED THIS, THERE'S CARPETS TO BEAT. THEN YOU'VE TO PACK YOUR BITS AND PIECES. WE'RE OFF TO THE SEASIDE TOMORROW.
THE SEASIDE! IS THE MASTER SENDING US ON HOLIDAY?
NO, OF COURSE HE ISN'T! WHAT DAFT IDEAS YOU GET! WE'RE JUST BEING TAKEN ALONG TO LOOK AFTER THE MASTER'S FAMILY WHILE THEY'RE ENJOYING THEMSELVES.
STILL, WE'RE BOUND TO GET A FEW CHANCES TO GO TO THE BEACH. OH, I'M SO EXCITED! I'VE NEVER SEEN THE SEA BEFORE!
Next day —
SOUTHPIER! SOUTHPIER!
THAT'S US! UNLOAD THOSE CASES, GIRL!
THE MASTER'S HIRED A COACH TO TAKE THE FAMILY AND THEIR LUGGAGE TO THEIR HOLIDAY HOME. *WE'LL* HAVE TO WALK. RIGHT UP A CLIFF IT IS, TOO!
Soon —
I'VE NEVER SEEN THE SEA BEFORE! OH! IT'S SO *BIG!*
OF COURSE IT IS! IT GOES ALL THE WAY TO AMERICA. NOW HURRY UP!

THERE'S SHOWS ON THE BEACH AND ALL KINDS OF STALLS. OH! I CAN'T WAIT TO GO THERE! I'LL GO ON MY FIRST HALF DAY OFF!
But —
ALL SERVANTS' HOLIDAYS ARE CANCELLED WHILE WE'RE AWAY. WE'RE TOO FAR AWAY FOR YOU TO VISIT YOUR RELATIVES.
OH — BUT I WANTED TO GO TO THE BEACH!
YOU HEARD THE MASTER'S ORDERS! NOW GET ON WITH SCRUBBING THAT FLOOR!
HOW CRUEL! WE'RE SO CLOSE TO THE SEA, BUT WE CAN'T ENJOY IT.
A few days later —
THE MISTRESS IS IN A RIGHT MOOD TODAY. OH, NO! SHE'S RINGING AGAIN!
GO AND SEE WHAT SHE WANTS, SADIE.
WASH THESE LACE GLOVES — AND DON'T DAMAGE THEM!
I'LL BE VERY CAREFUL, MA'AM.
Soon —
THERE! THEY'RE SPARKLING WHITE.
GO AND HANG THEM ON THE LINE, THEN. AND DON'T DALLY. I'VE OTHER CHORES FOR YOU TO DO.
I CAN SMELL THE SEA FROM HERE, BUT I CAN'T SEE OR ENJOY IT. OH, IF ONLY I COULD!

Suddenly —
OH! WHERE DID YOU COME FROM?
I'D BETTER GET THAT GLOVE BACK. HE MIGHT TEAR IT!
HERE, BOY! GIVE ME THAT GLOVE!
GOT IT!
OH, WELL DONE! YOU'VE CAUGHT MONTY!
WHO?
MONTY. HIS REAL NAME'S MONTMORENCY, BUT I CALL HIM MONTY FOR SHORT. HE'S A SWEET LITTLE THING, BUT HE KEEPS RUNNING OFF. I CAN'T CONTROL HIM.
THANK YOU SO MUCH FOR CATCHING HIM FOR ME.
IT WAS NOTHING. I REALLY JUST WANTED MY MISTRESS'S GLOVE BACK.
OH, NO! IT'S TORN!
YOU MUST LET ME GIVE YOU A REWARD.
IF YOU COULD TELL MY MISTRESS THAT IT WAS YOUR DOG WHO TORE THIS GLOVE AND NOT ME, I'D BE VERY GRATEFUL.

OF COURSE I WILL! BUT YOU DESERVE MORE THAN THAT. WHAT ELSE WOULD YOU LIKE?
I'D REALLY LIKE A DAY AT THE BEACH, BUT MY MASTER WON'T ALLOW IT.

But, the next day —
THE HONOURABLE SARAH WHITE HAS CALLED TO ASK IF WE CAN ALLOW YOU A DAY OFF. IT'S VERY TIRESOME, BUT HER FATHER IS A MEMBER OF THE HOUSE OF LORDS, SO WE SHALL HAVE TO AGREE.
WONDERFUL!

So, outside —
JUMP IN, SADIE! WE'RE GOING TO THE BEACH!
HOW LOVELY! I CAN HARDLY BELIEVE THIS IS HAPPENING!

Soon —
THE PIERROTS ARE SO FUNNY! *YOU* LIKE THEM TOO, DON'T YOU, MONTY?

OUCH! THE WATER'S FREEZING! SOMEONE OUGHT TO HEAT IT UP!

Later —
OH, DEAR — IT'S TIME TO GO HOME. I ALMOST WISH I HADN'T COME NOW.
WHY? HAVEN'T YOU ENJOYED IT?

OH, I'VE HAD A LOVELY TIME, MISS, BUT THAT MAKES GOING BACK TO WORK EVEN HARDER TO BEAR.
WHY DON'T YOU LEAVE, THEN?
PAPA SAYS WE NEED SOMEONE TO LOOK AFTER MONTY AS I CAN'T COPE WITH HIM. SO WHY DON'T I RECOMMEND YOU?
THAT WOULD BE WONDERFUL!
YOU'D HAVE TO FEED HIM, GROOM HIM AND TAKE HIM FOR WALKS — TO THE BEACH, OF COURSE. DO YOU THINK YOU COULD MANAGE ALL THAT?
OF COURSE I COULD!
EXCELLENT! I'M SURE YOUR EMPLOYERS WILL LET YOU GO WHEN I SAY IT'S PAPA'S WISH.
And, a few weeks later —
MY OLD MASTER AND HIS FAMILY ARE RETURNING TO LONDON. THEIR HOLIDAY'S FINISHED.
BUT *I'M* STAYING HERE AT THE SEASIDE — AND I'M NEVER GOING TO LEAVE!
THIS HAS BEEN MY HAPPIEST SUMMER EVER, AND IT'S ALL THANKS TO YOU, MONTY!
THE END

Who's the perfect boy for you? Find out in our fun quiz!

1 Describe your ideal boy.

A Good looking and trendy
B Good fun and friendly
C Kind and clever

2 How would you spend your dream date?

A On a romantic walk
B At a disco
C Doing something different — like ice-skating!

3 What kind of things do you like?

A Animals, books, nature
B Music, films, TV
C Clothes, shopping, dancing

4 How would your friends describe you?

A Fashionable and
B Adventurous and friendly
C Shy and sensitive

5 What do you like to do at weekends?

A Chat or play with friends
B Window shop in town
C Go swimming or cycling

6 If you received a Valentine card, how would you feel?

A Delighted
B Curious
C Embarrassed

7 Which of these do you like best at school?

A Art, drama
B English, nature studies
C Games, languages

8 At a disco or party, where can you be found?

A Dancing with boys
B Chatting with your friends
C In a corner, quietly watching what's going on

ANSWERS

Add up your score then check your conclusions for your perfect boy

	A	B	C
1	3	2	1
2	1	3	2
3	1	2	3
4	3	2	1
5	2	3	1
6	3	2	1
7	3	1	2
8	3	2	1

conclusions

8 → 13

You're quiet, kind and thoughtful and like boys who are sensitive and care about others. What they wear and how they look isn't very important. It's who they are and what they think that counts.

14 → 19

Your life's all about fun. You like boys who share your sense of adventure and aren't always worrying about their appearance. They've got to like having a laugh and trying new things.

You love fashion, so your boyfriend will have to as well. You like a boy who cares what he wears and has all the latest looks. You'll enjoy being seen at discos and parties looking perfect together.

THE FOUR MARYS, Cotter, Field, Radleigh and Simpson, were third form pupils at St Elmo's School for Girls. One morning, at assembly —

1998 IS OUR CENTENARY YEAR, AND THE GOVERNORS HAVE DECIDED TO MARK THE OCCASION BY HOLDING A WEEK OF VICTORIAN CELEBRATIONS. IT WILL FINISH WITH A GRAND EXHIBITION OF ITEMS COLLECTED DURING THE SCHOOL'S FIRST ONE HUNDRED YEARS.

YOUR TEACHERS WILL GIVE YOU MORE DETAILS. YOU MAY ALL DISMISS NOW.
VICTORIAN CELEBRATIONS SOUND FUN!
YEAH! BETTER THAN NORMAL LESSONS, ANYWAY!

The first lesson was needlework —
I'VE ALMOST FINISHED MY MINI SKIRT, VERONICA. ONE MORE LESSON SHOULD DO IT!
IT'S BRILL, MABEL! I THINK *I* MIGHT MAKE ONE TOO.

I SHOULDN'T BOTHER, COTTER. YOU NEED A MODEL FIGURE — LIKE MINE — TO CARRY IT OFF.

CHEEK!

THE SNOBS NEVER MISS A CHANCE TO BE NASTY.

PUT THOSE THINGS AWAY, GIRLS. WE'RE WORKING ON A *SPECIAL* PROJECT TODAY. MRS MITCHELL WANTS YOU ALL TO WEAR AUTHENTIC VICTORIAN COSTUME DURING THE CENTENARY WEEK, SO WE'RE GOING TO MAKE THEM IN NEEDLEWORK CLASSES.

HOW RIDICULOUS. WELL, *I'M* NOT DRESSING UP!

WE MAY HAVE TO *MAKE* THE THINGS, BUT MRS MITCHELL CAN'T FORCE US TO *WEAR* THEM! WE'LL REFUSE!

TRUST THE SNOBS! IT'LL SPOIL THINGS IF EVERYONE DOESN'T JOIN IN!

Soon —
OUR SKIRTS AND BLOUSES LOOK GREAT!
THEY'RE EXACT COPIES OF THE ORIGINAL ST ELMO'S UNIFORM. WELL DONE, GIRLS.
IT'S A PITY WE DON'T HAVE THE BOATERS AND BOOTS, TOO.

AH, BUT ELMBURY THEATRE HAS AGREED TO LOAN US SOME. YOU ARE TO GO THERE ON YOUR NEXT VISIT INTO TOWN, TO GET KITTED OUT.
HUH! WELL *WE* SHAN'T BOTHER!

The following Wednesday —
OPEN
THERE'S ROGER AND HIS MATES FROM ST BARTOPH'S.
HI! WHAT HAVE YOU GOT THERE?
HI!

The Marys explained —
THIS VICTORIAN LARK SOUNDS LIKE FUN!
WE THINK IT'S CHILDISH. WE'RE NOT DRESSING UP.

OH, BUT YOU SHOULD! VICTORIAN COSTUMES WOULD REALLY SUIT YOU.
DO YOU REALLY THINK SO?
YES! LONG SKIRTS WILL HIDE THEIR AWFUL LEGS!
I HOPE MABEL AND VERONICA DIDN'T HEAR HIM SAY THAT!

WE'D REALLY LIKE TO SEE YOU TWO ALL DRESSED UP! THE CENTENARY CELEBRATIONS ARE NEXT WEEK, AREN'T THEY? COULD YOU COME INTO ELMBURY NEXT WEDNESDAY TO LET US SEE YOUR COSTUMES?
OH! WELL, ALL RIGHT . . . IF YOU INSIST.

On Monday —
THIS IS GREAT! EVERYONE'S REALLY ENJOYING THEMSELVES!
EVEN MABEL AND VERONICA HAVE ENTERED INTO THE SPIRIT OF THINGS — THANKS TO ROGER!
OH! SHE DOESN'T LOOK VERY HAPPY.
WHAT'S THE MATTER? WHY ARE YOU CRYING?
I'VE JUST STARTED IN FORM IA. EVERYTHING'S SO BIG, AND I MISS MY TWIN SISTERS, MINA AND TINA.
YOU'LL SOON GET USED TO IT, DON'T WORRY. WHAT'S YOUR NAME?
ARABELLA.
THE FIRST YEARS MEET IN CLASS 14. THEY'RE A NICE CROWD, BUT IF YOU STILL FEEL LONELY LATER, YOU CAN COME AND SEE US. WE'LL BE AT THE TUCK SHOP AT FOUR O'CLOCK.
I WILL. THANK YOU!
GOOD FOR COTTY — SHE'S CHEERED ARABELLA UP A BIT. WE'D BETTER GET A MOVE ON, THOUGH. WE'RE GOING TO BE LATE FOR OUR FIRST LESSON.
SORRY WE'RE LATE, MISS CREEF.
BE QUIET! CHILDREN SHOULD BE SEEN AND NOT HEARD!
OOPS! I FORGOT WE'RE PRETENDING TO BE VICTORIAN ALL THIS WEEK!
PUT THOSE BOOKS AWAY, MABEL. WE SHALL BE WRITING ON SLATES.

WE'LL START OFF BY WRITING TODAY'S DATE — MAY 15TH, 1898.
OOH! THE CHALK'S MAKING A HORRIBLE NOISE!
MAY 15th 1898

At lunchtime —
DRY BREAD AND SOUP? WHAT'S THIS?
PLAIN VICTORIAN FOOD, MABEL, AND IT'S ONLY FOR ONE MEAL A DAY. YOU'LL GET A PROPER SUPPER. COOK WILL BE SENDING THE MONEY SHE SAVES TO A THIRD WORLD CHARITY.

HUH! I'D RATHER HAVE A PROPER SCHOOL LUNCH! NEVER MIND, VERONICA. WE CAN TELL ROGER AND THE OTHER ST BARTOPH'S BOYS HOW GENEROUS WE'RE BEING WHEN WE SEE THEM ON WEDNESDAY.
GOOD IDEA, MABEL! WITH THAT, AND SEEING US LOOK SO ELEGANT, THEY'LL BE SURE TO ASK US OUT!
I DON'T THINK SO, SOMEHOW!

When lessons finished —
HI! ARABELLA! HOW WAS YOUR DAY?
NOT TOO BAD. I FELT SORRY FOR ONE OF MY CLASSMATES, THOUGH. SHE HAD TO WEAR A DUNCE'S CAP AND STAND IN THE CORNER.
CRUMBS! THE FIRST YEAR FORM MISTRESS IS TAKING THINGS A BIT FAR!

Next day —
THERE'S NO HOCKEY TODAY, GIRLS. I'VE MANAGED TO BORROW THESE HOOPS, SO WE'RE GOING TO LEARN HOW TO BOWL THEM.
SOUNDS FUN!
Soon —
LOOKS LIKE FIELDY WOULD HAVE COME TOP IN SPORT ONE HUNDRED YEARS AGO, TOO!
I WIN!

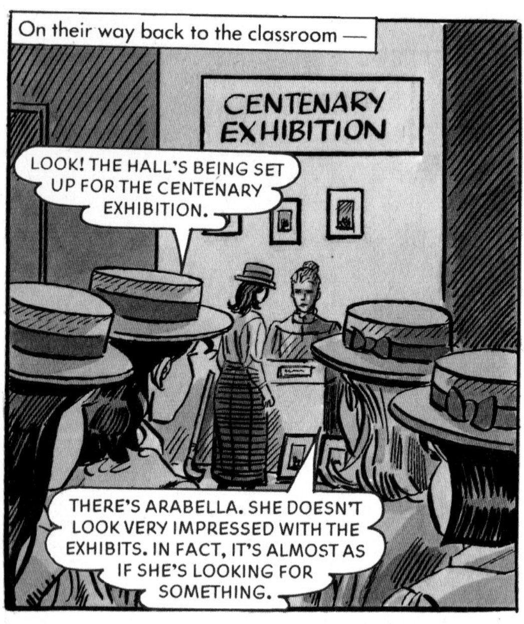
On their way back to the classroom —
CENTENARY EXHIBITION
LOOK! THE HALL'S BEING SET UP FOR THE CENTENARY EXHIBITION.
THERE'S ARABELLA. SHE DOESN'T LOOK VERY IMPRESSED WITH THE EXHIBITS. IN FACT, IT'S ALMOST AS IF SHE'S LOOKING FOR SOMETHING.

HI! YOU LOOK A BIT FED UP. HAVE YOU LOST SOMETHING?
ER . . . NO . . . I . . . I WAS THINKING ABOUT MY SISTERS AGAIN. LIFE'S NEVER DULL WHEN THEY'RE AROUND.

On Wednesday —
GOT STUCK IN A TIME WARP, LOVE?
HOW UNCOUTH! DADDY WOULDN'T EMPLOY PEOPLE LIKE THAT ON *HIS* BUILDING SITES.
I'M BEGINNING TO THINK WE SHOULDN'T HAVE COME INTO ELMBURY DRESSED LIKE THIS.

BUT ROGER ASKED US TO, AND — *AARGH!* MY HAT!

IT'S DRIFTING OFF DOWN THE RIVER! I'LL HAVE TO PAY FOR IT NOW!
NEVER MIND! IT'LL BE WORTH ALL THE HASSLE WHEN ROGER AND TONY ASK US OUT!

But, in the café —
OH — THERE'S NO SIGN OF THEM.
HAVE THE ST BARTOPH'S BOYS BEEN IN YET?

NO — THEY'VE ALL GONE AWAY ON A GEOGRAPHY FIELD TRIP THIS WEEK.
OOH! THEY MUST HAVE KNOWN THAT WHEN THEY ASKED US TO MEET THEM HERE. WE'VE BEEN SET UP!
HA! HA! IT SERVES THE SNOBS RIGHT!

On Friday —
ARABELLA'S FIRST WEEK IS ALMOST OVER. I WONDER IF SHE'S FEELING LESS HOMESICK NOW?
LET'S GO AND ASK HER.

But —
THAT'S ODD. WE HAVEN'T SEEN HER ANYWHERE.
LET'S ASK SOME OF HER CLASSMATES. THOSE GIRLS ARE IN IA.

ARABELLA? THERE'S NO-ONE IN OUR CLASS CALLED THAT.
BUT THERE MUST BE! SHE'S A NEWT. SHE STARTED THIS WEEK.
NOT IN *OUR* CLASS. WE'VE HAD NO NEW GIRLS SINCE LAST TERM.
SHE MUST BE DOWN IN THE BASEMENT.
WELL, SHE SHOULDN'T BE. IT'S OUT OF BOUNDS. WE'D BETTER GO AND FETCH HER.

I DON'T UNDERSTAND THIS! WHERE'S ARABELLA GONE?
OUT OF BOUNDS
WAIT A MINUTE! I CAN HEAR HER CALLING US!
COTTY! FIELDY!

But —
SHE'S NOT HERE. THERE'S JUST A LOAD OF OLD JUNK. PACKING CASES, PICTURES . . .
I DON'T BELIEVE IT! LOOK AT THAT PAINTING AND THE NAMES ON THE BOTTOM!
WE'D BETTER TELL MISS CREEF!
The following morning —
BEFORE I DECLARE THE CENTENARY EXHIBITION OPEN, MISS CREEF WOULD LIKE TO SAY A FEW WORDS.
LAST NIGHT, A PAINTING WAS DISCOVERED BY THE FOUR MARYS.
THE PAINTING IS OF THREE OF MY ANCESTORS WHO ONCE ATTENDED ST ELMO'S — TRIPLETS WHO DIED SOON AFTER THE PAINTING WAS COMPLETED. THEY'RE THE FIRST TRIPLETS TO HAVE EVER ATTENDED ST ELMO'S AND THIS IS THE ONLY PAINTING OF THEM ALL TOGETHER.
WHAT A TRAGIC STORY.
THE PAINTING HAS BEEN LOST FOR YEARS. IT WAS THOUGHT TO HAVE PERISHED IN THE GREAT FIRE OF 1899, SO THIS IS THE FIRST TIME I'VE SEEN IT. MRS MITCHELL SAYS IT SHOULD RIGHTLY BELONG TO ME, BUT I WISH TO DONATE IT BACK TO THE SCHOOL I LOVE.
THANK YOU, MISS CREEF. IT SHALL HAVE PRIDE OF PLACE IN OUR CENTENARY EXHIBITION!
I THINK THAT'S WHAT ARABELLA WANTED ALL ALONG. THAT'S WHY SHE LED US TO THE PICTURE.
SO WHO EXACTLY ARE THESE TRIPLETS, MISS CREEF?
MY GREAT AUNTS, MINA, TINA AND ARABELLA CREEF, ORIGINAL PUPILS IN 1898. I WONDER WHAT THEY WOULD HAVE MADE OF THE SCHOOL IF THEY COULD HAVE SEEN IT ONE HUNDRED YEARS ON?
ARABELLA, MINA AND TINA CREEF
LITTLE DOES MISS CREEF KNOW, BUT ONE OF THEM DID SEE IT! SHE WAS HERE FOR OUR CENTENARY WEEK. AT LEAST HER *GHOST* WAS!
THE END

Bunty
—A GIRL LIKE YOU
ARE YOU TWO COMING TO HELP ME CHOOSE A NEW WINTER COAT TOMORROW?
SURE!
YEAH, WE'LL MEET YOU IN TOWN.
So —
THAT'S NICE, BUNTY.
IT'S NOT REALLY WHAT I WANT, THOUGH. IT'S TOO LIGHT.
Then —
THAT'S GREAT, BUNTY.
YEAH, YOU REALLY SUIT IT.
NO, IT'S TOO DARK.
A lot later —
THIS IS THE ONE! IT'S JUST THE RIGHT SHADE OF BLUE.
WHAT DO YOU MEAN, BUNTY?
Back home —
I HAD TO GET A COAT THE SAME SHADE OF BLUE AS BUSTER'S SO THAT WE MATCHED!

DREAM ON!

SONIA BAILEY and her friends were trying to get on with new girl, Jenni Smith, but they were finding it difficult.

OOH, I JUST LOVE THOSE BOOTS! WHAT DO *YOU* THINK, JENNI?
I'VE ALREADY GOT SOME. THEY'RE IDENTICAL — WELL, MINE ARE PROBABLY BETTER — THEY CAME FROM A REALLY COOL SHOP IN LONDON.
GREAT FUN FASHION
Maths Jenni Smith
MATHS

I LIKE THE BAG.
I'VE GOT ONE LIKE THAT, TOO.

SHE WOULD HAVE!
OH, YEAH? HOW COME YOU DON'T USE IT FOR SCHOOL?
MY MUM LIKES ME TO DRESS PROPERLY FOR SCHOOL. THE ONE I WENT TO BEFORE WE MOVED HERE WAS VERY TRADITIONAL, YOU KNOW.

IT WAS A BRILLIANT SCHOOL, THOUGH.
OF COURSE!

JENNI'S A REAL PAIN, ISN'T SHE?
YEAH, WE'VE TRIED HARD WITH HER, BUT ANYTHING WE DO, OR SEE, OR BUY, SHE'S ALWAYS BEATEN US TO IT!
A few days later —
I'M REALLY NERVOUS ABOUT MY MUSIC EXAM TODAY.
IT'S VIOLIN, ISN'T IT? WHICH EXAM?

WELL, SO SHE SAYS . . .
YEAH — SHE LOOKED A BIT AWKWARD WHEN YOU POINTED OUT NO-ONE'S SEEN THAT BAG SHE'S SUPPOSED TO HAVE, AMANDA!
I KNOW! I BET SHE HASN'T GOT THE BAG AT ALL! OR THE BOOTS! SHE'S JUST LIVING IN A DREAM WORLD!

When Emma told her —
OH, IT'S EASY! I PASSED IT LAST YEAR.
YOU NEVER SAID. I BET MRS GREY WOULD LOVE TO HAVE YOU IN THE SCHOOL ORCHESTRA.

I HURT MY SHOULDER SO I'VE BEEN TOLD NOT TO PLAY FOR THE MOMENT.
HOW CONVENIENT!
DREAM ON!

Next day —
IT'S GOOD OF YOUR MUM TO GO AND GET US TICKETS FOR THE LIPZZ CONCERT THIS MORNING, SONIA.
YEAH! WE'LL PHONE HER STRAIGHT AFTER SCHOOL TO MAKE SURE SHE'S GOT THEM.

But —
SHE COULDN'T GET THEM! SHE WAS THERE REALLY EARLY, BUT THEY'D ALREADY GONE!
IS THAT THE LIPZZ TICKETS YOU WERE TALKING ABOUT EARLIER?

I DIDN'T SAY ANYTHING THEN BECAUSE I DON'T WANT EVERYONE KNOWING, BUT *I'LL* BE ABLE TO FIX YOU UP WITH TICKETS. YOU SEE — PAUL, THE SINGER, IS MY BROTHER.

WHAT? BUT YOU'RE JENNI *SMITH* AND *PAUL'S* SURNAME IS *SORREL*.
I KNOW — HE CHANGED IT. SMITH'S A BIT . . . ORDINARY. ANYWAY, I'LL PHONE HIM TONIGHT AND SEE WHAT I CAN DO.

Next day —
I TRIED PAUL LAST NIGHT, BUT COULDN'T GET HOLD OF HIM. THEY'RE ABROAD, YOU SEE, AND THE TIME DIFFERENCE MAKES THINGS DIFFICULT.
VERY CONVENIENT!

WHY DO YOU KEEP SAYING THAT? I *WILL* GET HOLD OF HIM.
YEAH — IN YOUR DREAMS!

A few weeks later —
RIGHT, I'VE SORTED EVERYTHING WITH PAUL FOR SATURDAY'S CONCERT. HE'S GOING TO LEAVE FOUR TICKETS AT THE BOX OFFICE, SO IF I MEET YOU WE CAN . . .
DON'T BOTHER, JENNI. WE'VE ARRANGED TO GO SOMEWHERE ELSE NOW.

I MEAN, WHAT'S THE POINT OF LISTENING TO HER DAFT STORIES?
YEAH! IF PAUL'S HER BROTHER, I'M THE QUEEN OF CHINA!

I DON'T THINK CHINA'S GOT A QUEEN, EMMA!
THAT'S WHAT I MEAN!

That Saturday —
DO YOU FANCY GOING TO THE HALL WHERE LIPZZ ARE PLAYING? I KNOW WE WON'T GET IN, BUT WE MIGHT SEE THEM ARRIVING OR SOMETHING.
YEAH, WHY NOT?

CONCERT TONIGHT
At the hall —
HEY, THERE'S JENNI!
BOX OFFICE
WHAT IF SHE *HAS* GOT TICKETS?

But, at the box office —
PULL THE OTHER ONE!
SEE? DREAM ON, AMANDA!
WELL THAT *PROVES* IT!
YEAH! JENNI'S BROTHER'S *NOT* IN THE BAND — JUST AS WE THOUGHT!

BUT IMAGINE TURNING UP AND ASKING FOR THE TICKETS! SHE REALLY MUST LIVE IN A DREAM WORLD.
HOW ABOUT GOING ROUND TO THE STAGE DOOR? MAYBE WE'LL SEE THE BAND THERE?

And —
THERE HE IS — IT'S PAUL!
AND LOOK WHO'S WITH HIM!
WHO? OUT OF THE WAY SO I CAN SEE!

STAGE DOOR
SORRY ABOUT THAT, SIS. IT'S BEEN A LONG TOUR. I FORGOT WHAT WE'D ARRANGED ABOUT YOUR TICKETS. COME IN THE BACK WAY WITH ME.
THANKS, PAUL!

STAGE DOOR
SO WHERE ARE YOUR MATES?
I DON'T KNOW. THEY COULDN'T MAKE IT FOR SOME REASON . . .
THE END

GREEN Scene

EVERYTHING YOU NEED TO KNOW TO MAKE THE WORLD A BETTER PLACE!

Don't Touch!

Not all baby birds or animals found on the ground will have been abandoned or be in need of help. If *you* find any next year, leave well alone. They may be being guarded by their parents who will be desperate for you to leave.

Water Waste

In winter, with rain and snow around, you're unlikely to think too much about saving water, but it's never too soon to start. Water is a very precious resource which shouldn't be wasted, yet we pour billions of litres away every year.

What can you do? Check out the list below!

1 Don't spend ages in the shower. Most people think showers use less water than a bath, but this is only the case if you shower for less than 5 minutes.

2 Turn off the tap while you brush your teeth.

3 Collect rainwater to pour on to your plants.

4 Don't overwater plants and when you *do* water them, do it when it's cool.

5 Use a watering can instead of a hose in the garden.

Feed The Birds!

Around half the British population feed birds in their garden during winter. If *you're* one of them, the R.S.P.B. asks that you make sure they're fed from a safe food source where cats can't reach them, that feeders are kept clean and free from old food, and water is fresh and not frozen. Follow these tips and you'll be rewarded by visits from *lots* of feathered friends.

BRRR!!

Keep cosy *without* wasting valuable energy!

★ Wear a hat! You lose a fifth of your body heat from your head. Check out the latest looks!

★ Exercise regularly. It'll boost your circulation and keep you fit.

★ Dress in layers. A few thin layers are much warmer than one thick one.

★ Recycle old tights and material and turn them into a dachshund draught excluder for your room!

Winter Wonders

Forest Enterprise sells around 250,000 traditional Christmas trees every year.

Chilterns Forest District has its own Christmas tree farm where 100,000 trees are planted every year.

Most of the trees sold are five feet tall and between five and seven years old.

Prince Albert introduced the custom of Christmas trees to Britain in 1844.

Deer! Deer! Deer!

All you need to know about Santa's helpers!

You'll find reindeer living around the North Pole in cold, dark conditions.

Luckily, they're well adapted to living there, with feet which are specially designed for walking in snow and slush.

Reindeer pull sleighs and provide people with transport in the Arctic.

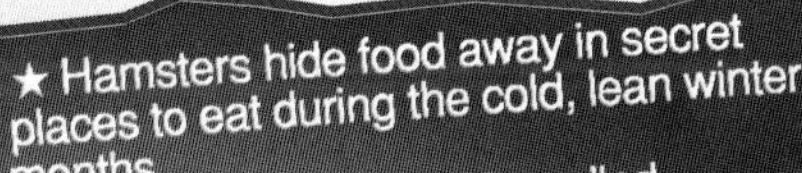

They have noisy joints which make an unusual 'clatter' when they walk.

You'll also hear them referred to as caribou.

Normally, reindeer live up to fifteen years, although some have lived to be over twenty!

In the famous story, Santa's eight reindeer were: Dasher, Dancer, Prancer, Vixen, Comet, Cupid, Donner and Blitzen. Rudolph was a later 'musical' creation.

How Green Is Your Garden?

Want to attract wildlife to your garden? The wider the range of plants grown, the more plants, insects, birds and mammals visit. So, if Mum or Dad are planning on adding to your garden or planting anything new, here are a few things to suggest.

NATIVE TREES — Birds need places to nest, roost and feed.

HEDGEROW SHRUBS — Again, these are good places for birds to nest. Prickly species — hawthorn and holly are especially good.

WILD PLANTS — Nettles, Bird's foot and Cuckooflower all provide food for butterfly larvae.

ORNAMENTAL PLANTS — Choose ones which will attract various insects. Honeysuckle for moths, buddleia for butterflies, etc.

GRASS — Leave some grass uncut the whole year if you can. This way, caterpillars won't come to harm through cutting.

Animal Magic!

★ Hamsters hide food away in secret places to eat during the cold, lean winter months.

★ Seals have a layer of fat called blubber to keep them warm in the cold sea.

★ Penguins love to 'toboggan' in the snow! They flop down on their tummies and push themselves along with their wings.

★ Hedgehogs can die when it gets too cold and they can't find enough to eat, so they hibernate when the weather gets cold.

★ Reindeer are the only deer species where females have antlers.

★ Penguins exist mainly on krill (tiny crustaceans) but also eat squid and, of course, fish!

PET PIN-UP
Bunty

SHARING SHANNON

IT was a big day for Amy Hall and Sophie Frazer — they were going to get a pony of their own.

Shannon

I HATE HAVING TO SELL SHANNON, BUT I'M JUST TOO BIG FOR HIM NOW.

DON'T WORRY, HE'LL HAVE A GOOD HOME WITH ME AND SOPHIE.

I CAN'T BELIEVE IT, SOPHIE! SHANNON REALLY BELONGS TO US!
I KNOW. IT'S GOING TO BE GREAT!

At the stables —
WHOSE PONY IS THAT, AMY? I HAVEN'T SEEN HIM BEFORE.
HE'S MINE AND SOPHIE'S. OUR MUMS HAVE BOUGHT HIM FOR US TO SHARE.

THIS ROTA IDEA IS BRILL! WE WON'T HAVE ANY ARGUMENTS ABOUT WHOSE TURN IT IS TO RIDE.
OR WHOSE TURN IT IS TO MUCK OUT THE STABLE!

Next morning —
HI, AMY. I GOT HERE EARLY, SO I THOUGHT I'D GET SHANNON READY FOR YOU.
OH — THANKS.
SOPHIE'S SADDLED HIM UP ALREADY. I WANTED TO DO THAT MYSELF!

Soon —
THIS IS GREAT. SHANNON JUMPS LIKE A DREAM.
DON'T TIRE HIM OUT, AMY — REMEMBER, IT'S MY TURN THIS AFTERNOON.

Suddenly —
STOP, YOU IDIOT! HE'S LOST A SHOE!

NOW I'LL MISS MY TURN TO RIDE!
SORRY. YOU'D BETTER HAVE BOTH RIDES TOMORROW TO MAKE IT FAIR.
I WISH SOPHIE WOULDN'T GET SO HUFFY. IT'S NOT AS IF I DID IT ON PURPOSE.

That evening, at Amy's house —
THAT WAS SOPHIE'S MUM ON THE PHONE. SHE THINKS WE SHOULD PAY THE BLACKSMITH'S BILL AS YOU WERE RIDING WHEN SHANNON LOST THE SHOE. I TOLD HER THAT WASN'T ON.

A few days later —
I CAN'T WAIT TO RIDE SHANNON AGAIN. FIRST WE HAD THE BLACKSMITH BUSINESS, AND SINCE THEN IT'S POURED WITH RAIN.

But —
SOPHIE, WHAT'S GOING ON? IT WAS *MY* TURN TO RIDE TODAY!
TOUGH! I MISSED MY TURN BECAUSE OF THE RAIN, SO *I'M* GOING NOW INSTEAD!

WE'RE GOING TO HAVE TO SORT THIS OUT. I WOULDN'T HAVE TAKEN SOPHIE'S RIDE UNLESS I'D CHECKED WITH HER FIRST.

Later —
LOOK! THE PONY CLUB IS HAVING A GYMKHANA.
I KNOW. I'M RIDING SHANNON IN THE NOVICE JUMPING — I SENT MY FORM OFF YESTERDAY.
CLUB
GYMK
THAT'S NOT FAIR. I'D HAVE LIKED TO HAVE GONE IN FOR THAT CLASS, TOO. I SUPPOSE I'LL HAVE TO ENTER THE SHOWING CLASS INSTEAD, BUT IT WON'T BE NEARLY AS EXCITING.

And at the gymkhana —
COMPETITOR NUMBER 44 IS DISQUALIFIED FOR HAVING THREE REFUSALS.
POOR SOPHIE — SHANNON'S JUST NERVOUS. HE'S NOT USED TO SHOWS.

BAD LUCK, SOPHIE. IT WAS A GOOD TRY. WOULD YOU GIVE ME A HAND GETTING SHANNON READY FOR THE SHOWING CLASS? THERE'S NOT MUCH TIME.
TOUGH! I'M OFF TO GET AN ICE-CREAM.

OH, WELL, IT LOOKS LIKE IT'S JUST YOU AND ME, SHANNON.

Later, in the showing ring —
CONGRATULATIONS, YOUNG LADY. A REALLY WELL TURNED OUT PONY AND RIDER.

OF COURSE, THE PRIZE WILL HAVE TO BE SHARED BETWEEN THE GIRLS. IT WAS PARTLY SOPHIE'S CAREFUL GROOMING THAT HELPED AMY WIN.
BUT AMY PAID TO ENTER, SO THE PRIZE IS ALL HERS.
OH, NO! EVEN OUR MUMS ARE ARGUING NOW!

BUT I BET SOPHIE WOULD HAVE KEPT THE LOT IF *SHE'D* WON! STILL, IT'S SILLY TO KEEP ARGUING OVER SHANNON. I'LL TRY AND MAKE A NEW START FROM TOMORROW.

But, next morning —
SHANNON'S GONE! SOPHIE'S TAKEN HIM AGAIN, AND SHE KNOWS IT'S MY TURN TO RIDE! RIGHT! THAT'S IT! I'M GOING TO SORT THIS OUT — I'LL GO AND SEE HER MUM *NOW!*

But, at Sophie's house —
AMY! I THOUGHT YOU'D BE OUT ON SHANNON. IT'S YOUR TURN TODAY.
BUT HE'S NOT THERE. I THOUGHT *YOU* HAD HIM!

Sophie's mum drove them to the stables —
DON'T WORRY, GIRLS. I'M SURE THERE'S A SIMPLE EXPLANATION.

But —
SHANNON? OH, YES — A MAN PUT HIM IN A HORSE-BOX THIS MORNING. HE SAID YOU WERE ALL GOING TO A SHOW IN THE NEXT COUNTY AND HAD TO MAKE AN EARLY START.
OH, NO!
WE'D BETTER GET THE POLICE.

Soon —
I'M AFRAID THERE'S BEEN A LOT OF PONY THEFTS IN THE AREA LATELY.
POOR SHANNON. I HOPE WHOEVER HAS GOT HIM IS KIND TO HIM.

Back at Sophie's house —
I FEEL SO AWFUL WITHOUT SHANNON, LIKE A BIT OF ME IS MISSING. THERE MUST BE *SOMETHING* WE CAN DO.
WE COULD TAKE A PHOTO OF SHANNON AND ASK ALL THE FARMERS IF THEY'VE SEEN HIM.

So, that weekend —
I DON'T KNOW IF IT'S HIM, BUT I DID NOTICE A CHESTNUT IN A FIELD NEAR ADDISON'S FARM LAST WEEK.
THANKS. WE'LL TAKE A LOOK.

But —
ANOTHER CHESTNUT PONY THAT ISN'T SHANNON. WE MUST HAVE SEEN A DOZEN SO FAR! *AND* RIDDEN MILES!
I'M WHACKED. LET'S GO HOME.

Later, at Amy's house —
SOPHIE'S MUM AND I HAVE DECIDED THAT, ONCE THE INSURANCE MONEY COMES THROUGH NEXT WEEK, WE'LL GET YOU BOTH ANOTHER PONY.
BUT I DON'T *WANT* ANOTHER PONY, MUM. I ONLY WANT SHANNON.

OH, SHANNON! EVERYONE ELSE SEEMS TO HAVE GIVEN UP ON YOU EXCEPT ME.

The following week —
I CAN'T WAIT TO CHOOSE OUR NEW PONY!
PONY SALES
POLICE
I JUST WANT SHANNON BACK. I ONLY AGREED TO THIS TO PLEASE SOPHIE.

THE BLACK PONY LOOKS GOOD. WHAT DO YOU THINK, AMY?
THAT OTHER PONY — IT — CAN'T BE, CAN IT?
I WON'T BE A SEC. I JUST WANT TO CHECK SOMETHING, SOPHIE.

IT *IS* YOU! THEY'VE DYED YOUR MANE AND TAIL, BUT I'D KNOW YOU ANYWHERE!

Just then, a man appeared —
ER — HOW MUCH IS THIS PONY?
I'D BETTER BE CAREFUL.
SORRY, MISS, THIS ONE'S SOLD. I'M JUST ABOUT TO TAKE HIM AWAY, BUT I'VE GOT PLENTY OF OTHERS BACK AT MY YARD.

Amy knew she had to act quickly —
I'VE FOUND SHANNON, BUT HE'S JUST BEEN SOLD!
IF YOU'RE POSITIVE IT'S SHANNON, AMY, WE'D BETTER MAKE SURE HE DOESN'T LEAVE.

HE'S PUTTING SHANNON IN THAT TRAILER.
RIGHT, I'LL TRY TO GET A POLICEMAN. YOU LOT BLOCK HIS WAY.

WHAT DO YOU THINK YOU'RE PLAYING AT? GET OUT OF MY WAY!
THAT'S OUR PONY IN THERE, AND WE WANT HIM BACK!

Just then, the police arrived —
WE CAN PROVE HE'S OURS, OFFICER — I ALWAYS CARRY THE CERTIFICATE OF OWNERSHIP — JUST IN CASE.
AND LOOK! YOU CAN SEE THE GOLD ROOTS WHERE HIS MANE'S GROWING OUT.

WELL DONE, GIRLS. WE'VE HAD OUR EYE ON THIS MAN FOR SOME TIME, IN CONNECTION WITH A SERIES OF HORSE THEFTS IN THE AREA.

WE'VE GOT SHANNON BACK AT LAST. I ALWAYS PRAYED THAT WE WOULD.

WE'VE DECIDED LIFE WILL BE EASIER WITH TWO PONIES. AMY CAN HAVE SHANNON AND YOU CAN HAVE THE BLACK PONY, SOPHIE.
OH, MUM — THAT'S BRILLIANT!
SHANNON'S GOING TO BE ALL MINE — I CAN'T BELIEVE IT!

The following day —
RACE YOU BACK TO THE STABLES, AMY!
RIGHT — COME ON, SHANNON!
HAVING A PONY EACH IS TWICE AS MUCH FUN!
The END

SILENT SCREAMS

"WE'RE off," cheered Clare as Dad drove the car out of the drive.

Her sister, Louise, joined in.

"We're going to a we-dding! We're going to a we-dding!"

Mum smiled. "Don't get too excited yet," she said. "We've three hundred miles to go, and the wedding's not until tomorrow."

"*That's* why it's exciting," said Louise. "We're looking forward to staying in a hotel tonight. It's like going on holiday."

It was their older cousin, Marianne, who was getting married at noon the next day. They would stay somewhere overnight on the way down and again on the way back.

Soon they were out of town and travelling past fields of cows, sheep and horses. The girls played 'I Spy' until they ran out of things to spy. They counted horses, people on bikes and tractors. But, after a few hours, they were bored and started to wriggle and grumble.

"How much longer?" asked Louise. "I'm tired of sitting in the car."

"Me, too," said Clare. "Can we stop soon?"

"We can start looking round for somewhere to stay the night," said Dad.

"Nothing too grand, mind. Just a nice, small hotel will do."

The girls perked up at this and began looking.

It was Clare who spotted it first.

"*There! Stop!*" she yelled.

Dad slowed down as Clare pointed to a swinging, wooden sign, which said THE POPLARS GUEST HOUSE, VACANCIES. Behind it, set well back from the road, was a lovely, old house.

Mum said she wasn't too sure but the girls pleaded with her.

"Please, Mum, let's stay here."

"They want us to stay — I *know* it," said Louise.

"What a funny thing to say." Mum laughed.

Dad smiled and said it was all right by him, so they turned up the drive.

Mum pointed out the big line of poplar trees at the back.

"I see why they called the house The Poplars," she said.

"Did you know people planted poplar trees to break the force of the wind?" asked Dad. "They grow very tall, you see."

"That's strange," said Mum as they got out of the car. "That sign's swinging, but there isn't a breath of wind."

"Maybe there's a little breeze down there," Clare said.

Before they could ring the bell, the door was opened by a smiling couple who introduced themselves as Jeff and Margaret. They called to their daughters, Linda and Julie, who came out to meet the guests.

"Look," said Jeff, "two girls of your own age to stay with us."

The girls looked pleased and their parents led the way upstairs to show the visitors their rooms.

"Come down when you're ready for a meal," said Margaret. "We want you to feel as if you belong here."

"How nice and welcoming," Mum said, when they'd gone.

"Did you notice Linda and Julie were wearing flared trousers?" asked Louise.

"They look like Mum in those old photos," said Clare. "They're nice though."

Soon the family was seated round the table having a delicious, hot meal.

"We love having people to stay," said Jeff, looking sad, "but nobody ever stays very long."

Later, Clare and Louise left the adults talking and went to play with Linda and Julie. Julie suggested they played

Monopoly, but Clare didn't think it was a good idea.

"It takes ages," she said. "We'll never finish the game tonight."

"It doesn't matter," said Linda, "as long as we enjoy ourselves. Besides, you might come back to stay again and we can finish the game then."

"That's silly," Louise protested. "You'll have put the board away."

Linda and Julie just smiled at each other.

"You'll see," said Linda.

They were allowed to stay up late, but they still didn't manage to finish the game.

Next morning, they got dressed in their best clothes for the wedding and were ready to leave straight after breakfast. Linda and Julie begged them to come back that night on their way home.

"The sign's still swinging," Mum pointed out as they drove off. "Very odd."

Clare and Louise looked forward to seeing their new friends again, but meanwhile there was the wedding.

Marianne looked lovely. The two girls threw confetti over her and her new husband as they were getting into the car to go to the reception.

They enjoyed the reception. It was a buffet — Louise had three helpings of strawberry trifle and Clare had four chocolate eclairs!

Soon it was time to wave goodbye to Marianne and Stephen as they set off on honeymoon for Portugal. After that, everyone started drifting away.

"I'm sad it's all over," sighed Louise.

"Me, too," said Clare. "But cheer up. It won't be long before we're back at The Poplars."

The girls were tired on the journey back, but they perked up when Dad said they were nearly there.

"It's just round this bend," called Louise.

But it wasn't. Nor could they find it round the next. Or the next.

"We've missed it somehow," said Dad. "We'll have to stay somewhere else instead."

"Let's go back and check, Dad. Ple-eease!" pleaded the girls.

But instead Dad turned down a lane which had a sign pointing to The Woodlands Hotel.

"We can't waste any more time," he said. "Sorry, girls."

They were shown to their room at The Woodlands. Louise went to test the springiness of the bed while Clare went to the window.

"Look," she squealed, "see the line of poplar trees? I don't know how we managed to miss the house but it must be there even if we can't see it from here."

Mum came to look.

"It's not far at all," she said. "The lane we turned down wound that way, so it must be just across the field there."

Louise begged and pleaded to go back, but Mum and Dad said they had booked in at The Woodlands, so they must stay. However, they agreed to let the girls go and visit Linda and Julie.

Clare and Louise took the path at the edge of the field and soon The Poplars came into sight. Just like before, the door opened as they approached and then they were inside with everyone smiling a welcome. They explained about Mum and Dad at The Woodlands, but Jeff and Margaret didn't seem to mind.

"It doesn't matter," said Margaret. "You're here now."

The Monopoly board was waiting and the girls were soon into the game again.

They played for a long time and Clare noticed Louise's eyes closing, just as she was feeling really sleepy herself.

She woke up to find Louise shaking her.

"Clare, wake up. It's morning. We've slept all night. Mum and Dad will be going mad, wondering what's happened to us."

Clare looked round in bewilderment at the bright morning sun shining through the window. Julie and Linda were by the window and called her over.

"Your parents are outside looking for you," said Linda.

"They'll be worried sick," said Clare, as she opened the window and called to them.

"Mum, Dad, we're here."

"They didn't hear you," said Louise.

Mum and Dad came nearer. Mum looked worried and Dad seemed puzzled, looking round as if dazed.

"Mu-um!" called Louise as Mum now stood right in front of her. But Mum just seemed to look through her.

"Mum, don't do that," said Louise. "Look at me. We're sorry. We didn't mean to worry you."

"Hang on, Louise. She doesn't seem to hear you and I don't think she's even seen you. This is crazy!" said Clare. "And listen — what are they saying?"

"I don't understand," said Mum. "There are the poplar trees, just as I remember. I'm sure this was where we stayed, and this was where the girls would have come last night."

"But they would have come straight back once they saw this ruin and realised they'd made a mistake," Dad replied.

Clare and Louise turned to stare at each other.

"*Ruin?*" spluttered Louise. "What *is* he talking about?"

"What is really strange," said Dad, "is what we found out this morning — that there *was* a place called The Poplars here, but it was gutted by fire in 1976."

"*What?* Where *are* we then?" Clare clutched Louise. They screamed at Mum and Dad, waving their arms wildly. But their parents, who were now just centimetres away, couldn't see them.

The girls turned to Jeff and Margaret, Linda and Julie. They were all smiling.

"People never usually stay long," said Margaret. "But you're here now. To stay — *forever.*"

THE END.

MAKE YOUR OWN...
CHRISTMAS CARDS
with these
SUPER STENCILS

MAKE THE STENCIL

Choose the design you want either from the ones shown below or pictures taken from old cards, wrapping paper, books and magazines. Trace the design onto tracing paper, then secure the tracing onto thin card (the sort used for postcards is about right), using masking tape. Carefully cut out your stencil with a sharp knife. Ask an adult to do this for you or to help you.

MAKE THE CHRISTMAS CARD

First buy or make envelopes, so that you know what size to make the cards. Also, don't use very thin paper for the cards or they won't stand up.

Using little pieces of masking tape, attach the stencil onto the card. Pour some paint into a saucer. Use quick-drying paint such as poster or acrylic paint. Dip your brush into the paint, then dab it onto a paper towel to get rid of excess paint. If you have too much paint on the brush it will run under the stencil. Holding the brush upright, dab the paint on until the shape is filled up. Carefully lift off the stencil and let your card dry.

A little verse inside and your card is complete!

WISHING MEL
SOMETIMES life seemed really unfair to Melanie Harper —
I LOVE GYM, BUT I'LL NEVER BE AS GOOD AS SAMANTHA! I WISH I WAS TALL AND SLIM LIKE HER, INSTEAD OF BEING SHORT AND PODGY!
DON'T TALK DAFT, MEL — YOU'RE NOT PODGY!
Later —
I WISH I HAD LONG, SILKY HAIR LIKE JUSTINE'S. MINE'S SO TUGGY!
BUT, MEL — YOU ONLY GOT YOUR HAIR CUT LAST WEEK BECAUSE YOU WISHED YOU HAD SHORT HAIR LIKE THAT NEW GIRL IN YEAR 10. YOU'RE *NEVER* HAPPY!
MARY JUST DOESN'T UNDERSTAND! EVERYONE ELSE SEEMS TO BE GOOD AT THINGS, OR LOOK BETTER THAN ME! *THAT'S* WHY I KEEP WISHING THINGS WERE DIFFERENT.
After school —
THE NEW PEOPLE ARE MOVING IN NEXT DOOR. IT WOULD BE GREAT IF THERE WAS SOMEONE MY AGE. BUT THAT WOULD BE TOO MUCH TO WISH FOR!
REMOVALS

THERE *IS* A GIRL! I'LL GIVE HER A WAVE.
SHE IGNORED ME! I SUPPOSE SOMEONE WHO LIVES IN A SEMI ISN'T POSH ENOUGH FOR HER! I WISH WE HAD A HOUSE LIKE THAT, THEN I COULD BE JUST AS SNOBBY!
But later, at Mel's —
IT WAS REALLY NEIGHBOURLY OF YOU TO INVITE US FOR A MEAL WHEN YOU HEARD OUR COOKER HADN'T BEEN DELIVERED, MRS HARPER.
NOT AT ALL. MEET MY DAUGHTER, MELANIE. I'M SURE SHE AND SUSAN WILL SOON BE GREAT FRIENDS.
HUH! IT'S THAT SNOOTY GIRL FROM NEXT DOOR.
HI! EXCUSE ME IF I PEER AT YOU, BUT I CAN'T SEE VERY WELL. ANYONE STANDING MORE THAN A FEW INCHES AWAY IS A COMPLETE BLUR.
SO SHE *DIDN'T* IGNORE ME WHEN I WAVED — SHE JUST DIDN'T SEE.
The two girls got on well straight away —
SUSAN WILL BE HAVING MAJOR EYE SURGERY SOON, WHICH MAY IMPROVE HER SIGHT. BUT, UNTIL THEN, SHE'S GOING TO FIND IT DIFFICULT GETTING AROUND A STRANGE PLACE.
I'M SURE MEL WILL TAKE CARE OF SUSAN, MRS WOOD.

Sure enough —
ICE RINK
YOU DON'T REALLY WANT ME AROUND WHILE YOU MEET YOUR FRIENDS AT THE RINK.
'COURSE I DO! ANYWAY, THEY'RE GOING TO BE *YOUR* FRIENDS, TOO, AND YOU SAID YOU'D NEVER BEEN SKATING, SO NOW'S THE TIME TO TRY.
Soon —
I WISH I HAD MY OWN SKATES INSTEAD OF HAVING TO HIRE THEM EVERY TIME, THEN I'D BE A BETTER SKATER.
YOU SEEM PRETTY GOOD TO ME. YOU MUST BE, TO STAY UPRIGHT WITH ME CLINGING TO YOU!
I WISH I COULD SKATE LIKE MARION! IT MUST BE REALLY THRILLING, GOING IN FOR COMPETITIONS.
IT'S ENOUGH OF A THRILL FOR ME JUST TO BE ON THE ICE, THANKS TO YOU, MEL!
Later, in the café —
OH, SORRY! I'M ALWAYS KNOCKING THINGS OVER!
DON'T WORRY, SUSAN. HEY, I'VE JUST SEEN THE REST OF THE GANG ARRIVE. COME AND MEET THEM.
Soon —
WE'RE ALL GOING TO THE YOUTH CLUB DISCO ON SATURDAY. COMING, MEL?
SURE! SUSAN CAN COME TOO.
A DISCO? OH, I — I DON'T THINK SO.
On the way home —
LOOK, YOU TRUSTED ME TO LOOK AFTER YOU AT THE RINK, SO WHY NOT COME TO THE DISCO?
WE-EL, IF YOU'RE SURE I WON'T BE BUTTING IN. YOU'RE REALLY LUCKY TO HAVE SUCH NICE FRIENDS, MEL.

So, on Saturday —
I'VE NEVER BEEN TO A DISCO BEFORE. I'M GLAD YOU PERSUADED ME, MEL.
JUST MIND YOU DON'T TRIP OVER SIMON'S FEET — THEY'RE BIG ENOUGH.
HEY, I HEARD THAT!
But next second —
WHOOPS — CAREFUL, SUSAN! I WARNED YOU ABOUT SIMON'S FEET!
IT WASN'T HIS FAULT. YOU'RE JUST MAKING EXCUSES SO I DON'T FEEL LIKE A CLUMSY IDIOT.
LOOK, RACHEL GRANT'S JUST ARRIVED — SHE ALWAYS LOOKS COOL. I WISH *I* COULD WEAR CLOTHES LIKE THAT!
I THINK YOU ALWAYS LOOK NICE, MEL.
I WISH MY MUM WOULD LET ME WEAR MAKE-UP . . .
UH-OH! SOUNDS LIKE WISHING MEL IS AT IT AGAIN!
At the end of the disco —
YOU LOOK TERRIFIC, KERRY! I WISH I HAD A TAN LIKE THAT IN WINTER.
I'VE BEEN SKIING IN SWITZERLAND. MY UNCLE'S GOT A CHALET THERE. WE'RE GOING AGAIN NEXT MONTH.
KERRY'S SO LUCKY — I WISH I WAS HER. I'VE GOT *NOTHING* TO LOOK FORWARD TO!
YEAH — WELL, I'M GOING NOW. 'BYE!

WHAT'S GOT INTO HER? I'VE NEVER KNOWN HER TO BE SO HUFFY BEFORE.
DID YOU MANAGE TO CHEER UP SUSAN, DEAR? HER MUM SAYS SHE'S GETTING NERVOUS ABOUT HER EYE OPERATION NEXT WEEK.
OH, NO! SUSAN NEVER TOLD ME. I'LL GO ROUND AND SEE HER TOMORROW.
Next morning —
SORRY I STORMED OFF LIKE THAT, MEL, BUT I JUST GOT ANNOYED WHEN YOU COMPLAINED ABOUT HAVING NOTHING TO LOOK FORWARD TO. I'D GIVE *ANYTHING* TO BE LIKE YOU. ALL *I* HAVE TO LOOK FORWARD TO IS AN EYE OPERATION!
I JUST DON'T UNDERSTAND WHY YOU'RE ALWAYS WISHING FOR THINGS TO BE DIFFERENT. YOU'VE GOT LOADS OF FRIENDS AND A GOOD PAIR OF EYES! I'D BE HAPPY WITH THAT!
I'M SORRY, SUSAN — YOU MUST THINK I'M A HORRIBLE, UNGRATEFUL PERSON!
NOT AT ALL! I THINK YOU'RE A TERRIFIC PERSON — YOU'VE BEEN SO KIND TO ME. SO DO ME A FAVOUR — STOP WISHING YOU WERE ANY DIFFERENT.
A week later —
EYE HOSPITAL
SUSAN MADE ME FEEL SO ASHAMED OF MYSELF! FROM NOW ON, I'M ONLY WISHING FOR TWO THINGS — THE FIRST IS THAT SUSAN'S EYE OPERATION IS A BIG SUCCESS, AND THE SECOND IS THAT WE'LL ALWAYS BE BEST MATES!
THE END

Knock Knock!
Who's there?
Rabbit.
Rabbit who?
Rabbit up neatly — it's Dad's Christmas present.

Get ready for laughs and groans with these beastly cracker jokes.

What did the stag say to his children?
Hurry up, dears!

What did the ram say to his girlfriend?
I love ewe.

Why did the bird sleep under the car?
To catch the oily worm.

Where does a lamb go for a haircut?
To the baa-baa shop.

Why do elephants paint their toe-nails red?
So they can hide in cherry trees.

What do monkeys sing at Christmas?
Jungle bells.

What dog has no tail?
A hot dog.

What do you get if you cross a cow and a duck?
Cream quackers.

What's a mouse's favourite game?
Hide and squeak.

What do you call a cat with eight legs?
Octo-puss.

What do penguins use to buy ice-cream?
Ice lolly.

What's the biggest mouse in the world?
A hippopota-mouse.

Why is a porcupine like a tailor?
Because it has lots of needles.

Why are camels moody?
Because they've always got the hump.

Why couldn't the butterfly go to the dance?
Because it was a moth-ball.

Where do Italian elephants live?
Tusk-any.

Why did the cow lie on the beach?
To tan her hide.

How do hens dance?
Chick to chick.

What bird is always out of breath?
A puffin.

Which snake is good at sums?
An adder.

Where do rabbits go after they get married?
On bunnymoon.

THE COMP
ON a cold, winter's morning, the pupils of Redvale Comp were making their way to school —
MATHS TEST THIS MORNING. YUCK!
WHAT WE NEED IS A MIRACLE, LAURA, TO SAVE US FROM IT!
WE SHOULD BE SO LUCKY, BECKY!
LOOK AT THOSE POOR SAPS, MORAG. OFF TO DO BASHER BARTLETT'S MATHS TEST! IF THEY WERE COOL, LIKE US, THEY'D BE DOING WHAT *WE'RE* DOING . . .
YEAH, SKIVING OFF, PIPPA!
BRRR! IT'S FREEZING IN HERE, HAYLEY!
THEY MUST HAVE FORGOTTEN TO TURN ON THE HEATING, LAURA!
At Assembly —
THE CENTRAL HEATING BOILER HAS BROKEN DOWN. UNTIL THIS CAN BE RECTIFIED, YOU WILL ALL BE SENT HOME. SCHOOL IS CLOSED FOR THE DAY!
YIPPEE!
IT'S OUR MIRACLE!
YOU WILL HAVE THE TEST TOMORROW NOW, SO I SUGGEST YOU USE TODAY AS A CHANCE FOR SOME REVISION. YOU COULD GO TO THE LIBRARY IN TOWN.
BASHER HAS *GOT* TO BE JOKING!
YEAH, LET'S HIT THE SHOPS, GUYS!

Claire and Nikki had other ideas —
WE'VE GOT OUR SWIMMING GEAR WITH US ANYWAY, SO I VOTE FOR THE LEISURE CENTRE! THEN WE CAN GO FOR A BURGER.
I'M WITH YOU, CLAIRE!
Meanwhile, in the record store —
HERE'S A MATHS PROBLEM FOR YOU, ROZ. YOU'VE GOT A MILLION POUNDS, SO HOW MANY POSTERS OF BOYZONE COULD YOU BUY?
FORGET THE POSTERS. I'D BUY BOYZONE! HA! HA!
Later, in the burger bar —
HOW DOES THIS SOUND, MORAG? 'DEAR MISS GRIMSTYLE, PLEASE EXCUSE PIPPA AS SHE WAS ILL ALL DAY YESTERDAY WITH A HEADACHE'!
BRILL! NOW, WHAT WILL I WRITE?
UH, OH! LOOK! IT'S CARTER AND JOHNSON!
GET DOWN! THEY MUST BE OUT OF SCHOOL FOR LUNCHBREAK — JUST OUR LUCK!
BUT WHAT ARE WE HIDING FOR?
BECAUSE THEY MUSTN'T SEE US, DUMMY! QUICK, THEY'RE LOOKING THE OTHER WAY. LET'S GET OUT OF HERE!
I HAVEN'T FINISHED MY CHIPS!

BUT *WHY* MUSTN'T THEY SEE US?
THEY'LL KNOW WE WEREN'T IN SCHOOL TODAY, SO WHEN WE HAND IN OUR 'SICK NOTES' TOMORROW, THEY'LL SHOP US!
That afternoon, in the park —
AMY! EMMA! HI!
LOOK WHAT KIKO'S HOLDING!
AW! HE'S SO CUTE!
WE FOUND HIM WANDERING LOST. THERE IS NO NAME ON HIS COLLAR, SO WE ARE GOING TO TAKE HIM TO THE POLICE STATION.
SOMEONE MUST BE MISSING HIM . . .
HEY! HODGE!
GOTCHA, BRADY!
GIVE ME BACK MY BAG!
CAREFUL, LAURA. IT'S ICY!
WHOOPS! OUCH!
SERVES YOU RIGHT!
HEY! WHAT WAS THAT NOISE? IT SOUNDED LIKE SOMEONE CRYING OUT . . .

Laura investigated —
OH! EVERYONE — COME HERE, QUICK!
IT'S ALL RIGHT — WE'LL HELP YOU. ARE YOU HURT?
LUCKY . . .
I'LL PHONE FOR AN AMBULANCE!
Soon —
PITY SHE COULDN'T TELL US HER NAME OR ANYTHING. SHE JUST KEPT SAYING LUCKY.
AMBULANCE
WAIT . . . WHAT ABOUT THE PUPPY? WHAT IF *HE'S* 'LUCKY'?
Laura and her mates hurried to the hospital —
MISS GOULD HAS CONCUSSION BUT NO BROKEN BONES. SHE CAN'T REMEMBER ANYTHING. WE GOT HER NAME FROM HER HANDBAG.
AND HER ADDRESS? COULD WE HAVE IT? YOU SEE, WE THINK WE KNOW WHERE HER DOG IS.
EXCUSE ME. YOUR NEIGHBOUR, MISS GOULD, DOES SHE HAVE A PUPPY?
WHY, YES — SHE DOES. LUCKY, SHE CALLS HIM.
SO, SEEING LUCKY MIGHT HELP MISS GOULD TO GET HER MEMORY BACK.
THEN LET'S GO AND RECLAIM HIM FROM THE COP SHOP!

Later —
I'M SORRY, I CAN'T LET YOU TAKE THE PUPPY ONTO THE WARD.
WELL, COULD YOU JUST SHOW US TO THE WINDOW OF MISS GOULD'S ROOM THEN?

And so —
MISS GOULD, LOOK — THERE'S SOMEONE TO SEE YOU.
LUCKY! MY — MY LITTLE LUCKY!

WE — WE WERE IN THE PARK. HE WAS TUGGING — THEN I SLIPPED.
SEEING LUCKY'S BROUGHT BACK HER MEMORY!

Next day, at Redvale Comp —
MISS GOULD'S NEIGHBOUR IS LOOKING AFTER LUCKY TILL SHE GETS OUT OF HOSPITAL.
I AM SO GLAD HE HAS FOUND HIS OWNER!
WHAT A DAY YOU LOT HAD! RESCUERS *AND* DETECTIVES!

HO! HO! YOU POOR CREEPS. ENJOY YOUR MATHS TEST YESTERDAY, DID YOU?
EH?
WELL, YOU MIGHT LIKE TO KNOW WE HAD A NICE DAY OFF BEING 'SICK'! SHAME YOU'RE NOT CLEVER LIKE US, ISN'T IT?

WHY ARE YOU ALL LAUGHING? WHAT'S SO FUNNY?
LET'S NOT TELL THEM. LET'S JUST WAIT AND SEE THEIR FACES WHEN BASHER HANDS OUT THE TEST PAPERS!
HA! HA! HA!
The End

Behind the scenes at BYKE

Filmed in an old mansion in the north east of England, Byker Grove must be the best known youth club in Britain. Unfortunately for the cast, it also has a school room, so none of them misses out on lessons when they're not on set acting!

To find out more and get all the goss, we took three of the stars, Kimberly, Gauri and Jody, to McDonald's for a chat.

Tell us how you got picked for Byker Grove

GAURI — My drama teacher asked me if I'd like to be an extra on Byker Grove, and I said yes. All I had to do was walk about in the background, not saying or doing anything special. The next day, the director asked me to do an audition. I read a bit of a script and they recorded my facial expressions. A couple of months later, I heard I'd got the part of Sita.

JODY — I did four auditions before I got my part as Cher. The first one was in the Tyne Theatre Stage School in Newcastle, where I go every Saturday. There were lots of other people auditioning with me but, gradually over the next three auditions, they eliminated the ones they didn't want.

Lots of things are considered before you get a part, including how well you will fit in with the rest of the cast and if your looks are different enough, so that the people watching won't confuse the characters.

KIMBERLY — My dancing teacher read about the audition. Unfortunately, the article was really old, so there were no parts left by the time I applied. However, the producer asked me to stand in for one of the girls. It was really boring because I had to stand around waiting for about ten hours.

I got an audition a few months later. That evening, when I was at dancing class, my mam told me I'd got the part of Karen — I was really happy.

What are you all like at school?

K — Hardworking and cheeky!

G — I am very friendly with everyone.

J — Quite loud, an okay worker, but some teachers call me disorganised.

And what's been your most embarrassing moment? The truth now!

K — Falling up the stairs in Fenwicks (posh Newcastle department store).

G — Falling on my bottom when I slipped on the snow — in front of loads of people at school!

J — Swinging my bag onto my shoulder and hitting a teacher in the face by mistake!

GROVE

So, what's the best thing about Byker Grove?

K, G & J — Making great, new friends — we all get on so well. We have a huge party at a place we all like when we finish filming the series and go out together to McDonald's like today. We get paid so we have money to spend on clothes and treats, though we are encouraged to save a lot of it.

IP+++HOT GOSSIP+++HOT G

. . a ghost of the White Lady haunts the tudio . . . none of the cast wear their wn clothes . . . most fancied boy — Chris Voodger (Noddy) . . . most ancied girl — Vicky Taylor (Angel) . . . he cast get bothered with loads of wasps in the summer . . . laughing, when you're supposed to be acting seriously, is the worst thing you can do — ever!

All About Me...

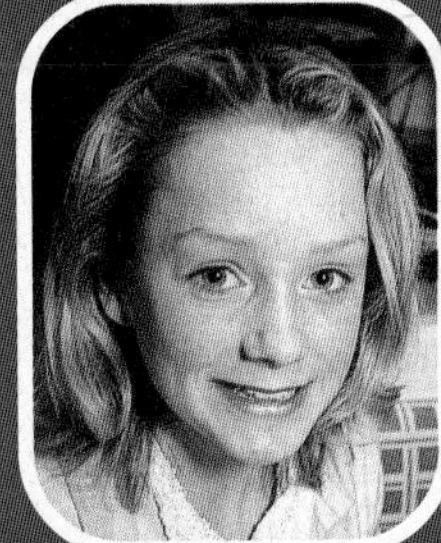

JODY BALDWIN
Byker character: Cher
Age: 15
Birthplace: Gateshead
Starsign: Gemini
Your first crush: Sylvester Stallone
Most fanciable man on the planet: Peter Andre
Most embarrassing record in your collection: Patsy Cline's Greatest Hits
Favourite music: Happy hard-core
Fave TV show: Fresh Prince
Favourite food: Seafood pizza
Pet hate: Chalk being scraped on the blackboard
Ultimate ambition: To be in a film with Jim Carrey or Sylvester Stallone
Hobbies: Jogging, acting, dancing, gymnastics and talking
Nickname: Gobby
Who would you like to swap places with for a day: Bette Midler

GAURI VEDHARA
Byker character: Sita
Age: 15
Birthplace: Newcastle
Starsign: Gemini
Most fanciable man on the planet: Paul Nicholls
What's the most embarrassing record in your collection: Bros
Favourite music: Mostly soul
TV fave: Friends
What's your happiest memory: When my niece was born
Favourite food: Cheese and tomato pizza
What is your ultimate ambition: To be an actress, singer, or dancer
What are your hobbies: Singing, dancing, acting and buying clothes
Nickname: Gug
Who would you like to swap places with for a day: Mariah Carey

KIMBERLY DUNBAR
Byker character: Karen
Age: 15
Birthplace: Newcastle
Starsign: Cancer
Your first crush: Jason Donovan
Most fanciable man on the planet: Scott Wolf
Favourite music: The Carpenters, Alanis Morrisette, Oasis and Louise
TV faves: Party of Five and Sister Sister
Happiest memory: Getting the part in Byker Grove
Fave food: Texan
Ultimate ambition: To be an actress or singer
Hobbies: Dancing, sleeping, watching TV
Who would you like to swap places with for a day: Louise Nurding

BUGSY
SANTA'S GROTTO
GLOOM!
SANTA BUG'S EATEN TOO MUCH CHRISTMAS PUD FOR LUNCH, BUGSY. YOU'LL HAVE TO TAKE HIS PLACE!
MALL MANAGER
YIKES!
So —
HELLO, LITTLE BUG! WHAT WOULD YOU LIKE FOR CHRISTMAS?
NOTHING! YOU'RE NOT THE REAL SANTA BUG!
YOUR ANTENNA'S NOT REAL — OH! IT IS!
OUCH!
Then —
HERE'S A PRESENT, LITTLE BUG.
HMM . . . IT LOOKS LIKE A TOY HAMMER.
GREAT! IT IS A HAMMER!
YOW!
Eventually —
WELL DONE, BUGSY! YOU SAVED THE DAY. HERE'S AN EXTRA BIG PRESENT FOR YOU.
ALL'S WELL THAT ENDS WELL. MERRY CHRISTMAS, EVERYONE!
CHOCS
Bunty
FOR GIRLS
CHOCS

merry christmas shopping!

It's Christmas every day of the year for Victoria Collins when she helps out at her mum's shop, The Traditional Christmas Shop, in the Metro Centre, near Newcastle. Victoria promised to show us round, so turn over the page to see what Santa might be bringing YOU this Christmas.

Victoria enters into the festive spirit as she invites us inside.

Victoria helps out as often as she can when she's not at school. Here she makes sure the shelves are well stocked.

A doll specially designed for the shop and named after Victoria.

An unusual gift — this Alice In Wonderland chess set.

Anyone would love this present — a talking monkey!

Victoria with a very special helper.

Everything's ready for the big day.

The end of another day at The Traditional Christmas Shop. Now, Victoria's off to do her own shopping. Merry Christmas, girls!

Bunty

Bunty
- a girl like you
BUNTY, WHY DON'T YOU WRITE OUT YOUR CHRISTMAS LIST? IT'S NOT LONG NOW, YOU KNOW.
OKAY, MUM.
NOW, WHAT CAN I ASK FOR? I KNOW — A CAMERA, BUBBLE BATH . . .
THERE YOU ARE, MUM.
FINE, BUNTY. LET'S HOPE FATHER CHRISTMAS HAS ALL THIS IN STOCK.
On Christmas Eve —
OH, NO! THERE'S ONE THING I FORGOT TO ASK FOR, BUT IT'S TOO LATE NOW!
And, on Christmas Day —
MY LAST PRESENT. COULD IT BE . . .?
YES! IT'S MY BUNTY ANNUAL! NO CHRISTMAS IS COMPLETE WITHOUT IT!
BUNTY

what's in a

Naomi

— means charming, delightful

Phillipa

— means someone who loves horses
variations Felipa, Philly, Pip, Pippa

Rebecca

— means faithful wife
variations Becca, Becky, Rebekah

Sandra

— variation of Alexandra, means defender
other variations Alexa, Alix, Sacha, Sondra

Pamela

— from the Greek word for honey
variations Pam, Pamella, Pammy

Sarah

— means princess
variations Sadie, Sally, Sara, Zara